T0309066

THE PUZZLE OF
SUSTAINABLE
INVESTMENT

LUKASZ POMORSKI

THE PUZZLE OF SUSTAINABLE INVESTMENT

WHAT SMART INVESTORS SHOULD KNOW

WILEY

For general information on our other products and services or for technical support, please contact our Customer Care Department within the United States at (800) 762-2974, outside the United States at (317) 572-3993 or fax (317) 572-4002.

Wiley also publishes its books in a variety of electronic formats. Some content that appears in print may not be available in electronic formats. For more information about Wiley products, visit our web site at www.wiley.com.

Library of Congress Cataloging-in-Publication Data is Available

ISBN 9781394226788 (Cloth)
ISBN 9781394226801 (ePDF)
ISBN 9781394226795 (ePub)

Cover Design: Wiley
Cover Image: © littleartvector/Adobe Stock Photos
SKY10074269_050324

For Hania, Gabi, and Lena

Contents

Acknowledgments

The views reflected in this book are mine, but they have been influenced by many insightful and generous people, coming from three broad and often overlapping environments.

First, I may not have dared to write this book if it weren't for the ESG investing course I taught at Yale University's School of Management and now teach at Columbia University's School of International and Public Affairs. I am very grateful to Toby Moskowitz and to Caroline Flammer, who invited me to teach at Yale and Columbia, respectively, and thus forced me to organize my thinking and lay out the evidence in a way that hopefully appeals to broad audiences. Marina Niessner and Eddie Watts were invaluable partners with the first editions of the course. To the many students who have taken the course: I thank all of you for our animated in-class discussions and for your pushing back and helping me refine my arguments. If I managed to convey my point clearly in this book, it is largely thanks to those interactions.

Second, I have been fortunate to practice what I preach at AQR Capital Management and at Acadian Asset Management. I have worked with so many talented researchers and portfolio managers at both these premier firms. At AQR, I had the support of the senior leadership team, most notably two of the firm's founders, Cliff Asness and John Liew, to lead the ESG research agenda and help address client needs, questions, and doubts about sustainable investing. I am very grateful to Antti Ilmanen for his mentorship, objectivity, and kindness—Antti, you set an example and a high bar that I keep trying to reach. A testament to AQR's culture and team spirit is the long list of coauthors I've had the pleasure to work with: Michele Aghassi, Paras Bakrania, Nicole Carter, Peter Diep, Jeff Dunn, Shaun Fitzgibbons, Andrea Frazzini, Jacques Friedman, Greg Hall, Bradley Jones, Kate Liu, Michael Mendelson, Christopher Palazzolo, Lasse Pedersen, Scott Richardson, Laura Serban, and Alice Zhao. Special thanks go to Steffen Bixby and Alfie Brixton, who were not only coauthors but also key partners on so many ESG projects. At Acadian, I am grateful for the involved conversations about ESG I've had with Brendan Bradley, Andy Moniz, Devin Nial, Ted Noon, Matt Picone, Seth Weingram, Fanesca Young, and Jerry Yu—I look forward to future joint projects with these and many other colleagues there.

Third, I have had the honor of speaking at many ESG investing conferences, sharing and debating my views with both the broader investment and academic community. In addition, the interactions with my colleagues on PRI's Hedge Fund Advisory Board, IIGCC's Hedge Funds and Derivatives Group, Qontigo's Sustainable Investment Advisory Board, and AIMA and MFA working groups were a wonderful learning opportunity and a chance to appreciate the wide range of approaches to sustainable investing. The complete list of meaningful interactions is much too long to include here. Still, I would like to mention at least the names of Michael Cappucci, Mark Carhart, Mike Chen, Harun Dogo, Peter Easton, Gifford Fong, Dave Larcker, Christian Leuz, Lubos Pastor, Don Raymond, Michael Simonetti, Johannes Stroebel, Bryan Tayan, and Jing Zhang, all of whom were partners or instigators of major ESG projects and whose views changed the way I think about sustainable investments.

In addition, I also thank the entire publication team at Wiley, with special thanks to Bill Falloon, Purvi Patel, Vithusha Rameshan, and Carol Thomas, who guided me through the process every step of the way.

And, last not least, I thank my family for bearing with me and supporting me throughout this project.

Chapter 1

Introduction

Over the past decade or so, sustainable investing went from a niche, little-known strategy to one of the hottest trends in the financial markets. The interest in this space led to trillions of dollars invested today in strategies managed with environmental, social, and governance (ESG)-related portfolio goals, or at least leveraging some of the information that warrants the "ESG" or the "sustainable" label. At the same time, sustainable investing has earned itself many critics who are deeply skeptical about its foundations and claims. Some of the opponents are forceful enough to argue for anti-ESG investing regulations, and such laws indeed get passed, notably by some US states.

You might hope that these conflicting ideas may be reconciled through a vigorous debate, but that seems unlikely. If anything, the views on sustainable investing are getting increasingly polarized and politicized. The proponents claim that this is the only reasonable way to invest, or a critical ingredient in achieving major environmental or social goals. The opponents denounce sustainable investing as an anti-capitalist plot that reduces investors' returns and maybe even harms the overall economy. Both these extremes are at least partly wrong.

Part of the problem is that commentators do not even agree on what the basic concepts mean and end up talking past each other. Sadly, this is not only the case between the two sides but also within them. For example, the proponents often meaningfully disagree about what constitutes sustainable investing and what does not. You may have noticed that in the first paragraph, I vaguely pointed to the "trillions of dollars" invested in this space. This is because the assessments, all from otherwise reputable sources, can range from $3 trillion to over $30 trillion.[1] As you will see shortly, I do not care for hyper-specific definitions of "ESG" or "sustainable" investing (I will use these

3

labels interchangeably throughout the book), but if a simple count of the assets involved can differ by a factor of 10, then we should expect even larger disagreements about more complex questions.

Another issue is that much of the commentary about ESG investing often reflects rather superficial analyses and sometimes outright muddled thinking. Again, this affects both sides of the debate. For example, both sides overstate the potential of using financial portfolios to influence corporate decisions. The pro-ESG crowd is banking on a large effect (and worries about greenwashing), the anti-ESG crowd fears it. If they thought carefully about the channels through which such impact might arise, perhaps we'd see less emotion and lower volumes in this conversation. The same holds for many other hotly debated questions, from the impact of ESG on portfolio returns, to the interpretation of ESG data, to what ESG even means once we go beyond investing in stocks and bonds. Ironically, many of these questions lend themselves to fairly straightforward economic analysis and can be addressed with clear and, in my view, persuasive economic intuition. Again, if we spent just a bit of time objectively thinking about these issues, we would likely end up much closer together than we are today.

I know that's a bold statement. If you are reading this book, you likely already know how heated the debate is, and you may be understandably skeptical about any conceivable consensus. Then again, consider that even the red states in the United States sometimes adopt ESG strategies. For example, in May 2023, the Florida State Board of Administration allocated $200 million to a fund focusing on clean energy and green transition; in September 2023, the Board announced that it committed to another renewable technology fund.[2] To put this in context, Florida passed a bill banning ESG investments by public funds; the governor of the state, who vocally supported the bill, is one of the Board's trustees. On the one hand, the Board made it clear that the investments were made strictly on the risk and return basis; on the other, most people would likely consider these new mandates ESG- or at least E-related. At the same time, some of the proponents of ESG investing are increasingly focusing on portfolio outcomes, not just on, say, how their portfolio may contribute to the global causes they care about. For example, in late 2022, the Oregon Public Employee Retirement Fund made a commitment to decarbonize their investment portfolio, which is a classic sustainable investing move. But when the State Treasurer made the pledge, he was very clear that it was solely based on financial considerations, notably climate risk that may affect the portfolio. The Treasurer added that the Fund's "investment decisions must be driven by financial considerations and investment returns, not politics."[3] So, perhaps there is a more balanced way to think about sustainable investing after all.

Which is precisely why I wrote this book. I believe that we have enough tools, frameworks, and economic intuition to allow a balanced analysis of this field and to see past the hot takes we often see in the media. We just need to accept that the answer to some of the critical questions will be the dreaded "it depends." I will try to make it up to the readers and at least explain what it depends on and how to assess which way a tradeoff may tilt in different environments and situations. As we do so, we will go over multiple case studies from investment practice. Moreover, I will strive to make the discussion as intuitive as possible and to avoid any technicalities and equations. Any interested reader with a basic grasp of economics will be able to follow the arguments. That's important, because you really can untangle most of the key disagreements in sustainable investing without resorting to esoteric arguments or combing through pages of mathematics. (In fairness, you may need them to translate the basic intuition into specific investment recommendations or policy advice, but do let's start with the basics first.)

This book reflects my years of experience designing and overseeing sustainable portfolios. I have had the privilege of working with investors who have a wide range of views on sustainability and often very different needs for their investment portfolios. What a blue state public pension may call "sustainable" can be dramatically different from what an endowment needs, let alone from the preferred approach for a Middle Eastern sovereign wealth fund. I've worked with plenty of institutions who were deeply skeptical and needed clear evidence that the only way ESG enters into their portfolio is non-concessionary: their positioning may reflect some ESG information, but only when it improves the purely financial investment view. These experiences taught me some humility and convinced me that there really are no silver bullets here. I intend to convey this in this book (well, at least the latter point).

In addition, I have been actively involved with and participated in working groups of multiple sustainable investor organizations, such as the PRI (Principles for Responsible Investment). This gave me a chance to work with other stakeholders, including other portfolio managers but also dedicated sustainability specialists who may not have an investment role, consultants, and, notably, ESG data vendors. This book will reflect what I learned not only through due diligence and rigorous testing, but also practical applications of such data.

Finally, and very importantly, I have translated my research and portfolio management experience into an ESG investing course that I have initially taught at Yale and, more recently, at Columbia University. The students are my "clients in the classroom" and are as important to me as the asset owners I may serve in my position within the financial services industry. Throughout the years, I refined my arguments. I had to, to be able to reach not just business or economics majors, but also the many public policy, sustainability sciences, climate, or forestry students who have been gracious enough to enroll in my course. I will apply these lessons in this book, which again aims at the broader audience, not just the specialists who already have ample investing or sustainability experience. (Even if I do believe that the specialists will learn something interesting from me, and I will help them by highlighting the parts of the book that they can safely skip.) And, just as in the classroom, I will be frank about the many tradeoffs and some outright shortcomings of sustainable investing. It is a fascinating and important field, but clearly not a panacea for all your investment and environmental and social needs.

What can you expect from this book? We will put ourselves in the position of an investor. This investor may well have sophisticated sustainability views and requirements, but we will focus strictly on how they map to the resulting investment portfolio. This means that many fascinating questions fall outside the scope of this book. For example, we will not debate policy. We won't ask whether a carbon tax is a good way to deal with global warming, although we will discuss how firms and security prices may react to a carbon tax if and when it is passed. Similarly, I will not try to explain how greenhouse gas emissions affect global temperature and lead to a host of other environmental and, eventually, also social effects. You and I may even disagree about this—which is completely fine as long as we both acknowledge that there are many investors who have a strong view on this question. And we will discuss how, given this view, such investors build their investment portfolios or how they may or may not be able to use their investments to influence the emissions of their portfolio companies.

We will begin with the single most frequently asked question in sustainable investing: does ESG help or hurt investment returns? One of my coauthors and former colleagues delights in answering this question with an emphatic "yes." And he's right. The question is ill-posed. To be able to address it, we first need to explain how investors actually incorporate ESG information in their portfolios and what financial and nonfinancial goals they want to express through their investments. We will see some of the key tradeoffs here and, importantly, will learn how to assess them in practice.

In Chapter 3, we will discuss how ESG information affects security prices. Our gut feeling may be that at least some environmental or social, let alone governance, characteristics should influence how much a company is worth. We will strengthen this intuition by discussing why that happens and through what specific channels this information impounds security prices. Importantly, we will also discuss markets in transition, thinking about the shifts in pricing when markets become more aware of ESG information, and maybe even push the prices further still to reflect the changing investor preferences. We will discuss how this affects the relationship between ESG and future expected returns, sometimes in ways that are counterintuitive at first, but are vitally important for investors building realistic investment views.

Chapters 2 and 3 will be relatively general in that the frameworks we will introduce hold for many different ESG issues, for different asset classes, etc. In these chapters, I will refer to some generic "ESG scores" without defining them further, other than in the specific investment case studies we will discuss. This changes in Chapter 4, which is all about ESG data. We will discuss the most obvious category of this data: ESG ratings that investors source from third-party providers. While some commentators are deeply skeptical about ESG ratings, I do believe they have important benefits for investors, even if these are not the obvious ones (such as predicting future returns). We will also talk about measuring specific issues within sustainability (for example, measuring a company's greenhouse gas emissions, as opposed to trying to come up with a single number summarizing all of ESG). We will end the chapter with a longer case study that explains how investors or researchers may design their own ESG measures, complete with a discussion of how we may want to test these to ensure that they actually capture what they were built for.

In all those early chapters, the main practical question is how to build a sustainable portfolio: which assets to buy and which to sell. That is clearly important, but for some investors, sustainability really begins only after your portfolio is already in place. So, in Chapter 5, we will discuss how investors interact with their portfolio companies, and will address the key question of whether one can meaningfully impact real economy activities through one's financial investments. I will provide evidence that impact is indeed possible, but I will also explain that it may arise through channels that many sustainable investors underappreciate. Moreover, I am cautious about the resulting magnitudes: investors can indeed have some impact, but we probably should be conservative in how much change they can actually effect. In Chapter 5, we will also review a relatively new sustainable investing security: green bonds (or labeled bonds more generally), and we will discuss some of their fascinating features.

Finally, in Chapter 6, we will go beyond the traditional asset classes of stocks and bonds. Until recently, sustainable investments started and ended with these asset classes. This should not be surprising. Stocks and bonds are relatively easier to analyze through the ESG lens, and they typically account for the vast majority of investors' portfolio allocation. Nowadays, this narrow view of ESG is increasingly untenable. Sustainable investors themselves are at least partly satisfied with the answers we already have for these traditional asset classes. Investors want to go further and think about ESG in their other allocations as well. In addition, the broader sustainable investing public, investor associations, and even the regulators want more than just stocks and bonds. Again, this is understandable. If an investor claims that they are "climate aware," you may want them to explain how climate affects their overall portfolio, and not just the 80% that the manager is more comfortable talking about.

Given this, we will show how the tools we developed earlier in the book can be applied to alternative investment techniques: first, shorting, and then the use of derivatives, especially commodity futures. The good news is that much of what we will have discussed by that point will still hold, even though there are nuances that we will need to control for. The bad news is that we may not always like the answers. During the many years I've spoken on responsible investing, I have rarely seen more emotion than when I talk about ESG and shorting or when I claim that shorting a company may actually have some impact on what the company does (the influence may be marginal, but still). This is also a rare occasion when discussions of reporting standards get close to violent. I will carefully review my arguments and will back them up with research published in top academic journals. I will try to convince you, but even if we disagree about how to interpret the evidence, I hope we only do so after analyzing the facts. We will close Chapter 6 with a discussion of yet another novel instrument: futures on carbon allowances, which give sustainable investors a way to invest in an important policy instrument that features prominently in many countries' decarbonization plans.

Before we start, an important caveat. The views that I present in this book are my own and do not necessarily reflect the views of my prior or current employers. Moreover, I will deliberately keep this book accessible to broad audiences and will avoid any technicalities or involved statistics, but whenever possible, I will point interested readers to where they may find such supporting evidence. These sources will sometimes include the research papers I have written over the years, but most of them have been through rigorous peer review and were tested by discussants and commentators at the conferences where I presented them. When I venture an opinion that I do not think can be validated by hard data, I will tell you so. Nonetheless, if any hidden mistakes or biases remain, they are mine alone.

With that out of the way, let's dig in.

Notes

1. For example, Morningstar's Global Sustainable Fund Flows: Q4 2023 in Review cites $3 trillion, while the sixth edition of the biennial Global Sustainable Investment Review reports US$30.3 trillion invested in sustainable assets globally.
2. Pensions&Investments, 1 May 2023, FSBA commits to clean-energy fund despite DeSantis' anti-ESG campaign, https://www.pionline.com/esg/florida-board-commits-clean-energy-fund-despite-desantis-anti-esg-campaign; FundFire, 25 September 2023, Florida SBA Invests in Another Renewable Energy Fund Despite State Ban, https://www.fundfire.com/c/4256184/547594?referrer_module=searchSubFromFF&highlight=florida%20invests%20in%20another%20renewable
3. As reported in *Responsible Investor*, 17 November 2022, https://www.responsible-investor.com/esg-round-up-oregon-public-employee-pension-fund-commits-to-net-zero/

Chapter 2

Does ESG Help or Hurt Investment Returns?

For most investors, a key objective is growing their capital by generating investment returns while limiting the amount of risk inherent in their investments. This simple statement is surprisingly potent and immediately suggests two ways in which sustainability may be useful for investors: it might point toward investments with higher potential returns or away from investments with higher potential risk. We will spend much of Chapters 3 and 4 discussing these two channels.

In addition to risk and return, some investors (and most, if not all, sustainability-oriented investors) will pursue other objectives in their portfolios. Such investors typically insist that portfolios reflect their values or nonfinancial goals. For example, the main portfolio objective may still be growing investment returns, but the investor may now only allow returns from a narrower range of securities. Typical examples include forbidding investments that are tobacco-related (e.g., stocks issued by tobacco producers) or investments related to fossil fuels (e.g., bonds issued by oil majors). But there are many more sustainability goals that investors pursue. They may want to manage their portfolio's climate exposure, for example, by putting a limit on the total greenhouse gas emissions their portfolio companies account for. Some investors may also want their financial portfolio to affect real economy outcomes, for example, by influencing the corporate decision making of the companies they invest in. We will discuss such objectives in much more detail in the coming chapters.

For now, I will refer to such goals and objectives as "ESG" or "sustainable." I will use these terms interchangeably, and I will not attempt to define them with any precision nor will I differentiate them from terms such as responsible investing, socially responsible investing (SRI), etc. In my view, ESG is a very broad umbrella term, and most people intuitively know when a piece of information, or a specific goal, falls within this category. When we start dissecting the category further, we lose the forest for the trees. For example, if news breaks that a company emits toxic sludge into the waterways, I will call that piece of news ESG-related, and I hope you will agree with that label. For our purposes, we do not need to further debate whether this is an example of the "E," "S," or "G" pillars of ESG. It may be Environment since the company may have damaged the local ecosystem; Social because the people may have ingested contaminated water; Governance because the incident was only possible because the captive board left the management unchecked and allowed it too many liberties. Similarly, I do not think it is fruitful to draw a distinction in how an investor may react to this incident if they follow sustainable investing versus an SRI approach. I acknowledge that different investors may react to this news differently (or, for that matter, that different data providers may adjust their ESG ratings differently). We will discuss such differences throughout this book. I just don't think we need to tailor a specific label for them.

With this in mind, let's begin with how ESG may affect portfolio outcomes, measured strictly in terms of risk and return. The bottom line will be that tradeoffs abound and that pursuing multiple goals, financial *and* nonfinancial, will generally detract from expected investment outcomes. This conclusion might be disappointing, but as we will see it is very realistic—which won't be surprising to those of us who have ever pursued multiple objectives in any activity, investment or otherwise.

Importantly, even this seemingly disappointing bottom line has a silver lining. As we will see, a portfolio built solely for financial outcomes will likely incorporate some sustainability information—what is referred to in the jargon as "ESG integration." Moreover, it turns out you can nudge the portfolio further toward your desired sustainability outcomes with only trivial investment consequences. That is, we may get a first-order improvement in the portfolio's sustainability characteristics with only a second-order reduction in expected investment attractiveness. This is great news, even if this holds only for a limited range of potential sustainability improvements. As we push the portfolio past that range, we will eventually start seeing meaningfully harsher investment penalties. We will then discuss the process through which investors could measure such degradation. This is an important part of the analysis in that it enables a more informed decision how to trade off investment versus sustainability portfolio outcomes. While the basic idea for this process, called the "ESG-efficient frontier," comes from an academic article, we will see examples of how real-world investors use it to build sustainability-oriented portfolio solutions.

Before we can do all of that, we will need to lay the foundation of portfolio theory. Readers who are already familiar with terms such as "mean-variance frontier" can safely skip the next section in this chapter. Those who may need a refresher should read on—keeping in mind my promise from the introduction that the discussion will be as non-technical as possible and will emphasize intuition over any formulas. To achieve this, I may need to glide over some nuances here and there—I do so deliberately, to be able to keep this section short and go back to sustainable investing soon enough. Readers who want a more rigorous, deeper dive are encouraged to consult one of many handbooks that focus on broad investments or portfolio theory.[1]

2.1 Portfolio Theory Refresher

Two key metrics of the financial attractiveness of investment portfolios are the prospective return (by how much we expect our capital to grow) and the investment risk (how much our capital may fluctuate or outright decrease over time). Not surprisingly, investors want to increase the former and decrease the latter. This intuitive heuristic holds across the various measures investors may use to capture these two quantities. For example, they may look at their portfolio return, measure it for the average year or for the whole period of their investment, consider the excess return they realize over some benchmark, etc. Their measures of risk may also vary, including well-established statistical measures such as the standard deviation or the variance of the returns they earn, but also metrics that only capture the downside risk (e.g., VaR, or Value at Risk), etc. For our discussion here, feel free to think about the simplest metrics, which for most people are total portfolio return and return standard deviation (often referred to as the return volatility). We will generally not discuss how investors may estimate these important metrics, other than discuss how ESG may enter into that process, which is something we will work on in Chapter 4.

To visualize the relationship between risk and return, investors often rely on risk–return charts that plot one against the other. Figure 2.1 is a typical example.

The horizontal axis in Figure 2.1 captures the investment riskiness of assets and portfolios, say their volatility. The vertical axis captures the expected return of the investment, measured as the change in the price of the securities you hold, relative to the purchase price and accounting for any dividends or other distributions you may have received in the meantime. For example, if you purchased a stock at $100 per share, held it until the stock paid a dividend of $10 and immediately sold the stock at $140, then your overall returns is ($140+$10−$100)/$100 = 50%. Importantly for Figure 2.1, it shows the return you expect to earn in the future, which might be informed by but generally will not be the same as the return you may have earned in the past.

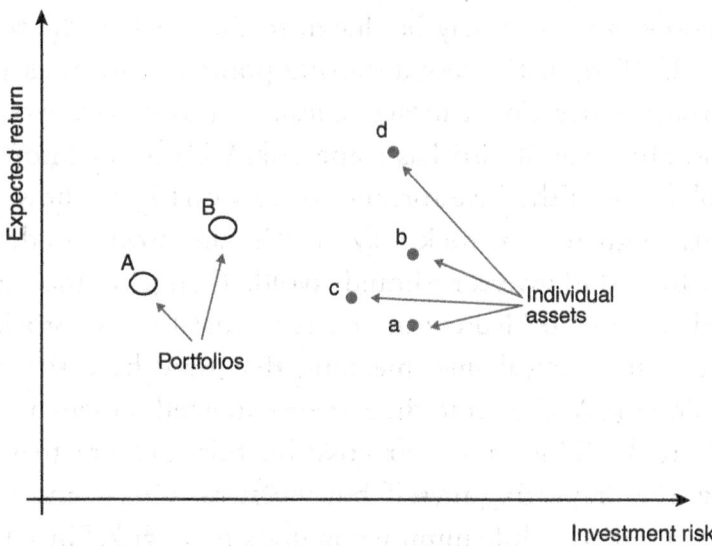

Figure 2.1   A stylized risk–return chart showing hypothetical individual assets and sample portfolios created from these assets.

Figure 2.1 shows a few individual assets the investor may consider investing in—if it is easier to visualize a concrete security, think about individual stocks you may trade in the stock market. Please note that each stock has its own expected return, reflecting how attractive you think that investment may be going forward, and its own volatility, reflecting how risky you think that stock is. There is an important relationship between at least some risks and expected returns, and we will touch on it in our next chapter. For now, let's just assume that we simply receive these quantities from a dedicated analyst.

An investor may choose to allocate all their capital into a single stock. It may not be the most prudent of investments, but may well be a possibility. In such a case, the individual stock's risk and return characteristics would also become the risk and return of the portfolio the investor holds. If an investor wanted to hold such a concentrated portfolio, which stock should he or she choose? Your eye may be drawn to the stock at the top of chart, "d." If so, that's a good starting point, as this stock gives you maximal investment attractiveness, as measured by expected returns. However, it also has some risk. We do not know the risk tolerance of the investor, and so we won't know how suitable that high-return stock may be. We can, however, identify stocks that the investor should avoid. Compare the stocks labeled "a" and "b." I drew the chart so that the two stocks sit on the same vertical line, meaning that they have the same portfolio risk. At the same time, their expected returns are different: stock "b" is more attractive on this measure than "a." I know I am repeating myself, but investors want to maximize expected returns while minimizing investment risk. Since these two stocks have the same risk, investors who try to decide between them should always choose "b" and never go with "a." In terms of its risk and return, "b" is a more efficient portfolio than "a" is. This conclusion is perhaps even more obvious when we compare stock "a" to stock "c." Note that "c" has both lower risk and higher expected return, so it is preferred over "a" on both these dimensions. Using a similar reasoning, we can also remove stock "b" from contention. This is because the highest expected return stock, "d," has a clearly higher expected return and, the way I drew that stock, slightly lower risk than "b."

At this point, we are down to stocks "c" and "d." Unfortunately, we cannot compare them as easily. On the one hand, "c" is safer, on the other, it also has a lower expected return. To proceed, we would need to know how much the investor is averse to risk (in the jargon, the risk aversion of the investor). If the investor is very risk averse, they would prefer "c" in spite of its lower return. If they are less risk averse, they will prefer the higher risk and higher reward stock "d."

So far, so good I hope. Let's now change gears and more from individual stocks to portfolios of stocks. Figure 2.1 shows a couple of sample portfolios, denoted with empty circles. I plotted these portfolios to convey important intuition about portfolio diversification. Portfolios composed of multiple assets tend to have less risk (are less volatile) than the individual assets included in these portfolios. In the chart, portfolios are well to the left of the individual assets to illustrate this point. The reason why this happens is that individual assets very rarely all move in tandem—their returns are less than perfectly correlated. Typically, some assets will go up in price, while some other assets might go down at the same time. Even if all assets move in the same direction, some of them will go up by more than others. What this means is that at least some of the risk of the individual assets you hold will be offset against the risk of other assets, and your overall portfolio will be less risky in consequence. This is great news to investors, to the point that diversification is sometimes referred to as the only free lunch one may have in investing. Some naysayers might argue that diversification guarantees that your portfolio will never do as well as the individual asset with the highest possible return. That's true, but diversification is still a great deal. It is next to impossible (or maybe just impossible) to precisely predict how well any single asset may do, so for the vast majority of investors, the right call is not to try and instead rely on what you can do much more easily: diversify at least some of your portfolio risks.

Coming back to our portfolios, which I labeled A and B. They both offer meaningfully lower risk than individual assets do, and their expected returns sit somewhere between the individual assets. The way we compare portfolios is very similar to the way we compare individual assets. In fact, we can extend this earlier argument and show that if we can invest in these portfolios, then an allocation of 100% of our capital in stock "c" is no longer attractive. This is because, on a standalone basis, this stock has both a higher risk and a lower expected return than either of the portfolios.

This basic argument is not enough, though, to eliminate either portfolio A or portfolio B or, for that matter, a standalone portfolio that invests 100% of our capital in stock "d." This is because the risk ordering of these portfolios ("d" is riskier than B, which is riskier than A) is the same as the ordering of expected returns ("d" is more attractive than B, and B is more attractive than A). Again, to proceed, we would need to know more about the risk aversion of the investor.

Two more insights before we come back to our sustainable investing discussion. First, from our discussion so far, an investment portfolio will be more attractive when it moves toward the northwest quadrant of the risk-return chart (so, up and to the left). This idea is captured in a variety of metrics summarizing portfolio attractiveness that divide a measure of attractiveness such as the expected return over a measure of risk such as volatility. Increasing such a ratio means that we are moving to the northwest in the chart, which is exactly what investors want. (If you can visualize a line from a point on the vertical axis toward the portfolio, such measures capture how steep that line is.)

The most famous, and arguably the most relevant of such measures is the *Sharpe ratio*. Formally, this ratio is defined as the ratio of the risk premium of a portfolio over the volatility of the portfolio. In turn, the risk premium is the difference between the expected return of the portfolio and the return of a riskless investment (e.g., a Treasury bill). We will discuss the risk premium in more detail in Chapter 3, but for now the important point is that the Sharpe ratio captures the risk-return tradeoff of a portfolio and that investors choosing between portfolios should go with the one that has the higher Sharpe ratio (and potentially balance it with the Treasury bill, if the standalone portfolio is too risky for them). We will rely on this heuristic shortly, in our discussion of the ESG-efficient frontier.

To round out our lightning-speed review of portfolio theory, let me make an important comment about portfolio. We discussed why an investor who wants to maximize return and minimize risk will not want to put 100% of their capital in a single stock such as "a" in our chart. The reason was that "a" offers an inefficient balance between investment risk and reward. There are portfolios of stocks that can get the investor more expected return at the same level of risk, or less risk at the same level of expected return, or maybe even both higher expected return and lower risk. It does not mean that stock "a" is unimportant. It may even be the case that stock "a," or other similar stocks, feature prominently in the composition of such efficient portfolios. The key insight here is that such stocks do not have attractive risk–return tradeoffs on their own, but they may bring valuable diversification benefit to an investor's broader allocation. Perhaps "a" has a negative correlation with returns of most other stocks—it pays off handsomely when most other stocks go down in price. Such rainy day insurance is extremely valuable to investors and they are usually willing to hold some portion of their portfolios in such assets even if they do not pay a high expected return. In fact, such stocks may be attractive in a portfolio even if we expect to lose money from holding them. This is for the same reason why most people hold insurance: we expect to lose money on insurance, on average, and yet we hold it, because it pays off at those times when disasters strike. As we will in subsequent chapters, this intuition also holds for some ESG considerations. There may be ESG investments out there that are not very attractive in terms of their own risk and expected return characteristics. These stocks may still be very important in an investor's overall portfolio if they tend to pay off at times when other stocks in the portfolio do poorly. We will see some such examples in the coming chapters.

2.2   ESG Integration

Let's start with a simple but informative thought experiment. Suppose there are two equally skilled portfolio managers, both supported by a talented research team, and both focusing on the same investments (say, US equities). Both managers seek to maximize financial returns, and minimize investment risks, just as we discussed in the previous section. There is only one difference between them. The first manager will refuse to look at any information that may have to do with sustainability. We'll label this manager "ESG unaware." In contrast, the second manager will consider any and all information that may be helpful to assess an investment, potentially including ESG. Let's call this manager "ESG aware." Here's the question: if you were to invest with one of these managers, who would you rather choose?

The answer is hopefully obvious. The ESG-unaware manager ignores some information that may be helpful in assessing stocks' risk and return characteristics. This means that the portfolio he or she comes up should be expected to be relatively inferior than that of the ESG-aware manager. That's not to say that the manager will necessarily lose money, or underperform some benchmark, etc. Perhaps the investor is so skilled, or able to process information so well, that the resulting portfolio is still attractive even if it ignores any possible ESG information. That's all fine—but the point is that the portfolio should not be expected to be *as attractive as* that of the second manager, who is equally skilled and who uses even more information to pick stocks. At best, if all ESG information is worthless for valuation or risk purposes, the two managers' portfolios should be equally attractive.

Of course, our thought experiment is somewhat contrived, but it captures powerful intuition: ESG is a source of information and some of this information may be helpful in pursuing investors' purely financial goals. This is true regardless of how these investors feel about ESG more broadly. We can illustrate this example using a risk–return chart of the type we introduced earlier in this chapter.

Figure 2.2 contrasts the portfolios of the first manager (ESG unaware) and the second one (ESG aware). As we discussed, the former may still be an attractive portfolio, offering high returns given its risk. But the second portfolio will, in general, be more attractive, offering higher returns, or less risk, or both (as depicted in the chart). We now know how to read this chart. In our simple but powerful risk–return framework, investors would always prefer the ESG-aware portfolio relative to the ESG-unaware one.

Incorporating ESG into one's views of risk and return is referred to as ESG integration. The intuition we've just developed suggests that ESG integration is a good thing—it helps us build a

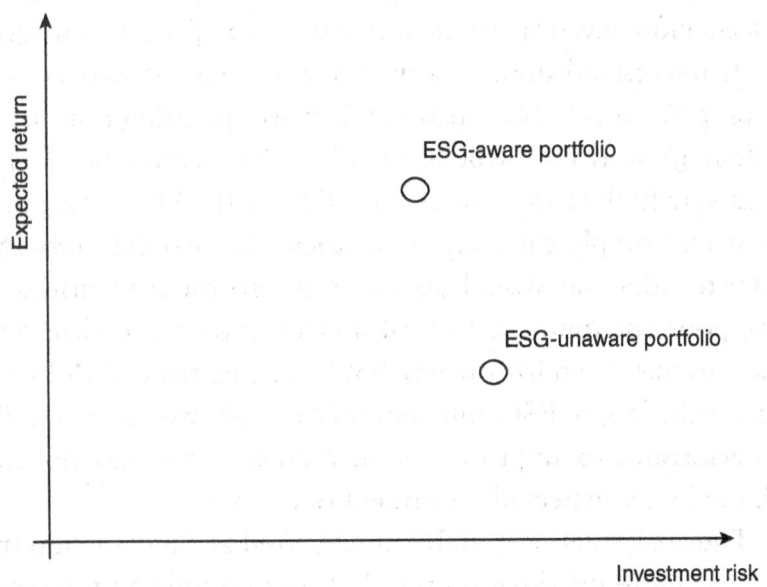

Figure 2.2   ESG integration: using more information may improve expected risk and return outcomes.

better portfolio. It is difficult to imagine situations in which investors would *not* want to do that. This statement is quite general, although I smuggled in one additional assumption: that at least some ESG information matters for risks or returns. Without that assumption, the portfolios of the two managers would be identical. That is, the ESG-aware investor above would rationally decide not to act on any such information and would build a portfolio that's identical to that of an ESG-unaware investor. This may well be the case for some investment strategies. For example, high-frequency trading (HFT) or statistical-arbitrage portfolios open and close positions within very short periods (a day, or a week) and over such short horizons ESG insights might hardly matter. With such strategies, all managers may as well be ESG-unaware.

Having said that, the assumption that at least some ESG information matters seems reasonable. The next chapters will discuss a variety of evidence showing that some aspects of ESG may indeed allow investors to identify attractively priced securities or better understand these securities' risk profiles. Moreover, while at this point it is only a nuance, it is worth pointing out that our analysis above is valid whether ESG predicts returns positively or negatively. In the latter case, the portfolio of the ESG-aware investor would simply tilt away from stocks that exhibit "pro-ESG" characteristics and would instead lean into those securities that have poor environmental, social, and/or governance characteristics. This may seem like an anti-ESG investing stance, but I would argue this, too, is ESG integration. After all, we are using ESG characteristics to improve our investment view and hopefully achieve better expected investment outcomes.

The analysis above can be summarized as "information matters and more information should lead to improved investment outcomes." This statement is true when applied to ESG but also any other type of information.

And finally, it is important to stress that our analysis deals with *expected* investment outcomes. The insights above hold on average, and as such are important for investors building portfolios. But we should also keep in mind that actual realized investment outcomes can differ from our expectations. It may happen that the portfolio of an ESG-unaware investor does better than that of the ESG-aware one in any month, quarter, or year, for reasons as prosaic as luck. The fact that you used more information does not protect you, in investing or in any other field, from randomness.

Let's consider a non-ESG example that will help us understand this better. Imagine a home buyer—or perhaps think back to when you were considering buying a house. To assess your potential investment, you likely looked at a host of information, including the layout of the house, its age, the neighborhood it is in, etc. Now, suppose you needed to buy a house but for some reason could not access some information: for example, you could examine the layout of the house but could not see the neighborhood it is in. Would you choose the same house in either situation? Probably not—it is likely that at least some features of the neighborhood are going to be important for you, and you would not want to willingly ignore such information. If you did, the choice you'd make can be expected to be relatively inferior. It's not to say that you'd necessarily buy a horrible house—it's just that you should expect to identify an even better one if you had more relevant information at your disposal. More information is better, at least unless you're convinced from the get-go that the information is worthless (and if you are, I will do my best in the next chapters to un-convince you).

The above example, contrived though it is, also helps us understand why our point about ESG integration holds for expected investment outcomes and is clearly not a guarantee. Compare the two houses from before: the one you chose with all available information, and the one you chose without seeing the neighborhood. You can rightly expect that the former is a better fit for you. But can you guarantee that you'd still feel this way a year after you move in? Perhaps the first house seemed nicer but has some hidden faults that you simply could not see upon the initial inspection. Perhaps the neighborhood is not as attractive as you initially thought, but you could only realize that after living there for a while. This does not mean that you made a mistake in deciding on the house. It is possible that you were simply unlucky in that the faults, or the neighborhood's shortcomings, were not apparent or could have been deemed unlikely, based on the information you had at the time. You still made the right decision based on the information you had and on your expected outcome, it's just that the outcome that transpired diverged from the expectations.

2.3   Incorporating ESG Preferences in a Portfolio

So far, we have discussed how investors may leverage ESG information to improve their understanding of investments' risk and returns. That is important, but many ESG investors insist on more. They may also require that their portfolios exhibit attractive ESG characteristics, perhaps relative to some benchmark. A typical example may be building the portfolio while avoiding securities the investor considers unethical (say, tobacco stocks) or aiming to arrive at a portfolio holding stocks with greenhouse gas emissions substantially lower than those of the broader market.

Unfortunately, we cannot rely solely on ESG integration to achieve these objectives. This is because portfolio decisions may utilize some ESG information, but are also likely to incorporate a host of other data. These other considerations may outweigh

ESG inputs in the investment process. For example, the investor may believe that carbon-heavy companies may not be attractive investments in the long run. But perhaps the investor sees attractive tactical opportunities in at least some carbon-heavy companies—for example, perhaps such companies might be extremely attractively priced, have strong fundamentals, long-term contracts with their customers, etc. These tactical considerations may win out, at least some of the time. In fact, even if the investor outright restricts stocks of (say) the 10% of the biggest emitters, their portfolio may still have a relatively unattractive climate profile if the tactical investment view likes the next 10% of heavy emitters.

To avoid such situations, investors build constraints into their process. This is not a new technique, or a technique necessarily associated with sustainable investing. Traditional constraints would prevent a portfolio from (say) building a concentrated position in a single sector or country. An ESG constraint, in contrast, may prevent the portfolio from having any holdings in tobacco, from building an excessive portfolio-level carbon ownership, etc. (We will delve deeper into at least some such goals in later chapters.) ESG-type goals and objectives, and the resulting portfolio constraints, are a key part of sustainable investing. For some investors, they are simply nonnegotiable—for example, when investors' ethical views dictate which companies are prohibited in the portfolio.

The need for such constraints is clear even when ESG information is deemed to correlate with investment attractiveness and directly enters into investors' risk and returns views. When this happens, we may expect that the portfolio that integrates ESG will naturally avoid unwanted "sin" exposures, delivers the desired green profile, etc. But, at least some of the time, this simply won't be the case. At such moments, the constraints reflecting ESG objectives will bite and will force the investor to alter the portfolio. Such alterations, unfortunately, will lead to at least marginally inferior expected risk and return outcomes.

This important point may seem subtle, so we will introduce another thought experiment to explain it in more detail. As before, let us consider two portfolio managers. As before, the two are equally skilled, have the same resources at their disposal, etc. Unlike before, we will allow the two managers to use the same information, whether ESG-themed or not. The difference between the managers is that the former can invest in any security he or she chooses, whereas the latter has a strict ESG mandate that excludes any tobacco, fossil fuel, or controversial weapons producers. The question is: which manager should be expected to deliver better investment outcomes?

As before, the answer is hopefully clear to most readers. The first manager may find attractive investment opportunities in the tobacco, fossil fuel, or weapons industries and will incorporate them into their overall portfolio. The second manager may be able to identify the same opportunities but, working with the strict ESG mandate, will not be able to act on them. Thus, their portfolio will not be as attractive. At least some of the time, the second manager will leave some valuable investment opportunities on the table. This does not mean that the manager will necessarily underperform some benchmark—the resulting portfolio can still be well positioned, but the point is that it should not be expected to be *as attractive as* that of the first manager.

A different way of thinking about this is to ask yourself whether there is some level of valuations at which tobacco, fossil fuels, or weapons companies would be financially attractive. The answer to this question must be "yes." We might think that these companies are unethical, that their products hurt the society or the environment, or maybe even that they will go bankrupt very soon, when their negative externalities become obvious to all investors. However, these companies may well produce cash flows and earnings in the meantime. For example, even if the overall economy is slowly moving toward net zero carbon, countries such as China or India still purchase coal, giving profitable business to coal mines, if only temporarily.[2] This means that the underlying business is worth *something* (more than zero) and security prices should reflect that value. If prices drop below that level, then the security becomes an attractive investment opportunity. The point of our second thought experiment is that some investors, such as our second manager above, would not be able to purchase these securities *at any price*, no matter how cheap they become. Since the second portfolio manager will pass on at least some such investment opportunities, the first manager necessarily should be expected to produce superior expected performance.

As before, this reasoning holds for expected risk and returns. There is no guarantee that the first portfolio manager always produces higher returns, every quarter, year, or decade. Randomness again may drive realized performance away from expectations. For example, the incredibly cheap coal mine the first investor bought might get flooded, its customers might renege on their contracts, etc. The first manager, who allocated capital to the coal mine will then suffer a loss. The second manager, not having invested in the coal mine, avoids the pain. Importantly, such negative outcomes may have been anticipated before making the investment, they just were not perceived to be particularly likely—if they had been, the investment would not have been attractive, and the first manager would not have undertaken it.

Finally, some readers may have noticed that I tried to add "financial" and "risk and returns" to our discussion. This was deliberate. I cannot claim that the first manager is better than the second one, or that hiring the first manager would always be the right choice for asset owners. Far from it. For many investors, the first manager is not even an option—they would never consider investing in a portfolio that might expose them to, say, tobacco, even if that portfolio only holds tobacco some of the time. Some investors may agree to a small reduction in expected performance to avoid the headache. Of course, to make an informed decision here, we would first need to assess the magnitude of this reduction. This is where the ESG efficient frontier comes in.

2.4   ESG-Efficient Frontier

We will now combine the intuition explained in the prior sections into an elegant theory that allows investors to combine their financial and nonfinancial goals and formally assess the impact of the latter on the former.[3]

To explain this, we need to be able to compare the "ESG-ness" of various portfolios. This is a daunting challenge, and we will consider it from many different angles in Chapter 4. For now, we will simply state that there is some metric that captures what investors care about when they think about ESG or the sustainability of their portfolios. This might be something as simple as "no tobacco in the portfolio" or as complex as measuring the potential impact the portfolio companies have on society or the environment. For the following charts, we will assume that higher scores are better, meaning that portfolios that have higher values of our metric also have more attractive ESG characteristics that the investor cares about.

In addition to the ESG metric, we will also need to measure the purely financial attractiveness of an investment portfolio. As we remember from the beginning of this chapter, investors seek to improve their returns while limiting the risk their portfolio is exposed to. We also learned about a useful measure that relies on both these quantities: the Sharpe ratio, which captures how much return investors earn per unit of risk. While our discussion below holds for other portfolio attractiveness measures, we will focus on the Sharpe ratio, given its straightforward intuition and its widespread use in the investment industry.[4]

With these preliminaries, we're off to the races. Let's start with formalizing the intuition behind ESG integration we discussed earlier in this chapter. Figure 2.3 does that, illustrating the portfolios of the two portfolio managers from our first thought experiment: the one ESG-aware manager, who uses all available information, and the ESG-unaware one, who refuses to consider any ESG information.

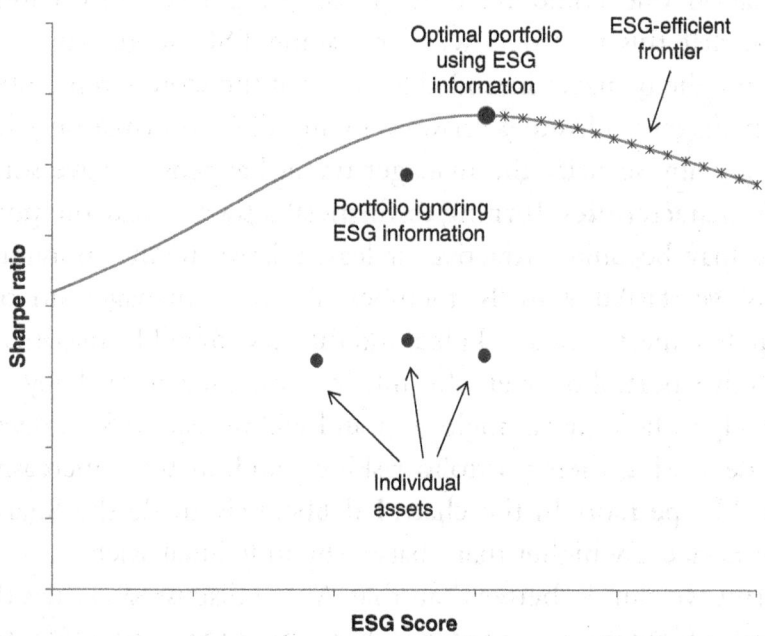

Figure 2.3 ESG-efficient frontier: maximal portfolio attractiveness for any desired sustainability score.

Source: Pedersen, L., Fitzgibbons, S., and Pomorski, L. (2021). Responsible investing: the ESG-efficient frontier. *Journal of Financial Economics*, 142 (2): 572–597.

Figure 2.3 is conceptually similar to the risk-return diagrams from Figures 2.1 and 2.2, but different in that it now introduces a measure of sustainability. It is represented on the horizontal axis as a portfolio's "ESG score." The vertical axis is the Sharpe ratio, combining measures of risk and expected returns in a single quantity capturing a portfolio's investment attractiveness. The chart starts with individual assets, or the building blocks we use in portfolios—think stocks, or bonds, or perhaps other securities. Each individual asset has some ESG score (for example, a company's standalone sustainability profile) and some measure of financial attractiveness (the risk–return tradeoff of a portfolio invested 100% in that one asset).

Let's look at the ESG-unaware manager's portfolio: the best allocation one could build while ignoring ESG information. Note that this portfolio will have some ESG score. This isn't because the manager intended to arrive at the score—remember, the manager is blissfully unaware of any ESG information—but because any security the manager trades happens to have some ESG characteristics. Turning to financial attractiveness, the portfolio may be quite attractive, at least relative to the individual assets we started with. Remember that both managers in our thought experiment are skilled, and they try to build a maximally attractive portfolio given the information they have. They are unlikely to hold just a single asset and will instead seek to diversify, decreasing their portfolio riskiness and, in turn, increasing their Sharpe ratio. In the chart, I deliberately made the Sharpe ratio noticeably higher than that of the individual assets.

But we can do better than that. As we discussed earlier, the more information a manager has, the more attractive the expected performance of the resulting portfolio. The ESG-aware manager also considers ESG information, which improves the Sharpe ratio of the resulting portfolio, moving it up in our chart. The chart additionally allows us to measure the magnitude of improvement: how much the addition of ESG-type information may help a portfolio's financial returns. Measuring the improvement (the financial value of ESG integration) is challenging in practice—after all, few portfolio managers would willingly ignore information that might otherwise be useful to their process. We will attempt to at least approximate it in Chapter 4, by looking at how strongly different pieces of ESG information help us predict prices.

In Figure 2.3, I plotted the ESG-aware portfolio up and to the right, indicating not just the improved Sharpe ratio but also suggesting the portfolio has more attractive ESG properties. This is an assumption that we have not needed so far in our analysis. Whether we talk about integration or the impact of portfolio ESG goals, our reasoning holds whether better ESG characteristics are associated with higher expected returns or whether the opposite is true. In the latter case, the ESG-aware manager would simply build an "anti-ESG" portfolio that emphasizes securities with poor ESG profiles. In fact, we will consider such situations in Chapter 3, when we discuss how ESG investing may lead to the formation of a "sin premium," or relatively higher expected returns from holding securities with poor ESG scores. In Chapter 4, we will discuss plenty of examples in which ESG information correlates positively with expected returns, as I depicted in Figure 2.3.

Figure 2.3 also helps us illustrate the impact of ESG considerations. Think back to our second thought experiment. We compared two managers who access all information, including ESG. The first one attempts to build a portfolio with maximal financial attractiveness—the portfolio with the highest Sharpe ratio, already depicted in Figure 2.3. The second manager has the same information, but also needs to ensure that the portfolio achieves some ESG objectives. We do not need any additional assumptions to decide where this portfolio sits relative to the first one. We know that the manager seeks an improvement in the ESG score, so the portfolio will be to the right. We also know that adding ESG objectives detracts from financial attractiveness, reducing the Sharpe ratio and moving the portfolio down in the chart. The benefit of putting these portfolios in a chart is that we can try to measure the changes in sustainability scores and in the resulting Sharpe ratio. Measuring the tradeoff should help investors make better, or at least more informed, portfolio decisions. Unlike with integration, this measurement is more straightforward in investment practice, and we will see some real-life examples shortly.

Before we do, let's stay with our second thought experiment and think about how the second manager would know how much sustainability is enough. In some situations, this will be relatively clear: for example, the portfolio may have zero tolerance for tobacco. In general, though, things are not as easy. If investors seek green portfolios, should they ask the manager to deliver at least a slightly lower carbon exposure? Or perhaps at least 25% lower than the overall market? Or 50% lower? There is no obvious answer here.[5]

In Figure 2.3, there are many possible portfolios that optimize both financial performance and sustainability. They are denoted with asterisks, to the right of the portfolio maximizing the Sharpe ratio alone. Each portfolio on that line segment delivers highest financial attractiveness for a given portfolio ESG score. Ideally, the investor would make the decision based not only on the preference for sustainability but also based on the risk and return implications. For example, if a major improvement in sustainability requires only a paltry reduction in the Sharpe ratio, then perhaps we should insist on such a major boost. If some ESG needs are costlier in that they reduce the Sharpe ratio more meaningfully, then perhaps we should be satisfied with a relatively lower improvement.

But how do we know how much is enough? Heuristically, we could start with any given level of sustainability and then attempt to build the best possible portfolio that would achieve precisely that ESG score. We can then target a slightly higher ESG score and again look for the best possible portfolio for that ESG score. If we keep doing that, we will eventually build the ESG-efficient frontier, or the set of all portfolios that deliver the financially optimal risk–return ratio for any level of sustainability preferences. Figure 2.3 plots such a frontier, showing the maximal risk–return tradeoff investors could hope to attain for any desired level of sustainability. The only suboptimal portfolio depicted in this chart is the allocation of the ESG-unaware manager from our first thought experiment. The chart shows that managers who swear off any ESG information are doubly handicapped. Not only is their Sharpe ratio lower than that of the "optimal" portfolio, but it is actually below the curve. What this means is that investors who are open to utilizing ESG information can build a portfolio with very similar sustainability characteristics (the same ESG score) but with a strictly higher Sharpe ratio.

There is one more powerful insight we will tease out of Figure 2.3. The chart shows that there is a single portfolio that has the highest attainable Sharpe ratio. This is not an assumption but rather a general result in portfolio theory, going back to the seminal work of Harry Markowitz. We won't go into more details here, but will instead focus on ESG implications. This highest Sharpe ratio portfolio has some level of sustainability— it might even be quite high, depending on the relationship between ESG characteristics and expected returns. This portfolio will be chosen by all investors who want to maximize their financial outcomes but do not have any preference for ESG.

Investors who care about both financial outcomes and ESG might only need some minimal level of sustainability, which might be satisfied with the same portfolio—in which case, we would be done. More interestingly though, a preference for ESG will move the investor to the right along the ESG-efficient frontier in our chart: the investor will trade off some decrease in financial attractiveness for an increase in sustainability.

Amazingly, Figure 2.3 suggests that this may be a very cheap tradeoff in that some initial increase in ESG might only cost a tiny decrease in financial attractiveness. To see this, notice that the curve is relatively flat around the "optimal" portfolio. (Calculus-inclined readers can think about what happens to the derivative at the maximum Sharpe ratio portfolio.) The flatness means that a small step to the right of the optimal portfolio will only marginally decrease the Sharpe ratio. This means you may be able to attain a first-order improvement in sustainability with only a second-order deterioration in financial performance.

Unfortunately, this argument only holds in the close neighborhood of the "optimal" portfolio. Eventually, the drop in the curve will become more pronounced. In other words, the more sustainability we need, the higher the penalty to the risk-return tradeoff. In practice, the drop will depend on the specific sustainability goal the investor is interested in.

Let's turn to a real-world example of such a goal. Many investors seek to build green portfolios, aiming to reduce the carbon emissions of their portfolio companies below the carbon emissions of the overall market (usually, a benchmark index). Figure 2.4 shows how this goal interplays with financial attractiveness in a similar fashion as Figure 2.3 did. The horizontal axis in Figure 2.4 shows the amount of carbon reduction versus the benchmark, starting with portfolios at most as carbon-heavy as the benchmark on the left-hand side of the chart, with 50% of benchmark carbon emissions in the middle, to no carbon whatsoever at the

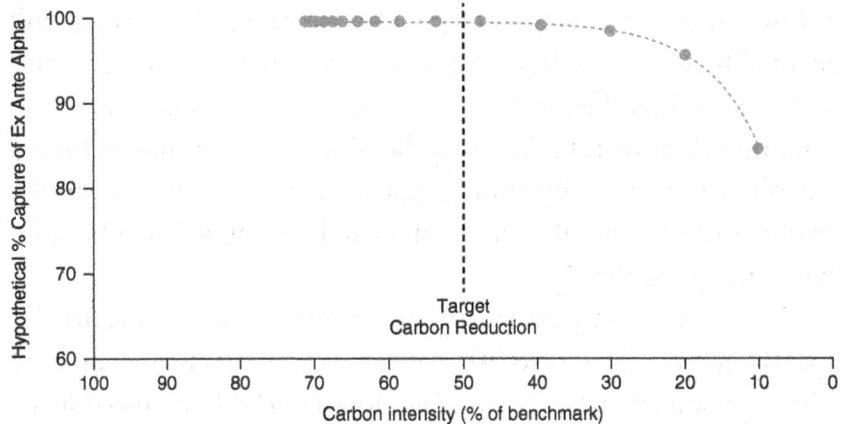

Figure 2.4   ESG-efficient frontier of a carbon-aware portfolio.
Source: Responsible asset selection: ESG in portfolio decisions. (2019). AQR
whitepaper.

far right. The vertical axis is a measure of financial attractiveness.
Instead of showing the level of attractiveness for each hypothetical portfolio, Figure 2.4 scales everything to the attractiveness of
the "optimal" portfolio, of the sort the ESG-aware manager
would build.

The first portfolio plotted in Figure 2.4 is precisely such a
portfolio, or optimal portfolio using all information, including
ESG, with no ESG constraints. Interestingly, this portfolio already
delivers some carbon reduction, at about 75% of the benchmark's
emissions. This might be because at least some of the investment
insights embedded in the portfolio point toward stocks with a
relatively greener profile than the benchmark overall.

As we move to the right, portfolio emissions drop more and
more: 70% of the benchmark's level, 60%, 50%... We are on the
flat part of the ESG efficient frontier, just as we saw in Figure 2.3.
Greening up the portfolio seems remarkably easy: reducing the
carbon ownership by 20% relative to the initial portfolio seems
to have a trivial effect on financial attractiveness, which remains

at almost the same level as before. This is not a fluke—as we will see in Chapter 4, carbon emissions are extremely lumpy and only a small handful of stocks account for the majority of the benchmark's emissions. We may be able to materially reduce a portfolio's emissions by simply not holding a couple of stocks, possibly out of many hundreds that can be included in a broadly diversified portfolio.

However, as we push on to the right the curve eventually dips. Reducing carbon to 30% of benchmark emissions already reduces financial attractiveness by close to 5% of its initial level; a reduction to 10% of benchmark emissions costs about 15%. Not surprisingly, many investors prefer to stay away from these levels and instead target a reduction between say 25% and 50%: meaningful, but perhaps defensible as requiring only a very modest reduction in the risk–return tradeoff.

Notes

1. The classic textbook choice is Bodie, Z., Kane, A., and Marcus, A.J. (2013). *Essentials of Investments*, 13e. McGraw Hill.
2. For example, Reuters newswire on 27 November 2023, China's thermal coal imports jump, crowding out India, https://www.reuters.com/markets/commodities/chinas-thermal-coal-imports-jump-crowding-out-india-russell-2023-11-27/
3. The discussion here is based on Pedersen, L., Fitzgibbons, S., and Pomorski, L. (2021). Responsible investing: the ESG-efficient frontier. *Journal of Financial Economics*, 142 (2):572–597.
4. Benchmark-aware long-only investors may prefer the "information ratio" rather than the Sharpe ratio. Our discussion generalizes to that measure as well, and the intuition we discuss in this book is equally powerful in that case.

5. In some situations, the required thresholds may be defined by regulation. For example, EU regulation on Paris-aligned portfolios specifies how much carbon reduction such portfolios should initially exhibit and at what annual pace they need to further de-carbonize their holdings.

Chapter 3

How Does ESG Affect Asset Prices?

erhaps the most frequently asked question in this entire field is whether ESG helps or hurts returns. We have considered this question already in the last chapter, discussing how ESG information and ESG objectives may influence financial outcomes. But so far, we kept the discussion at a very high level, never explaining why exactly ESG information may be helpful in building a better portfolio. We take this question head on here. We will start with a broad discussion of what determines security prices in the market, building a framework that we will then apply to sustainability. In the next chapter, we will test our insights on a variety of practical examples, borrowed from practitioner and academic literature on the topic. But before we do, we need to review some basics of asset pricing—as before, readers who are already comfortable with these concepts should feel free to just skip the next two sections.

3.1   Prices, Cashflows, and Discount Rates

What matters for asset prices, and how can we explain changes in prices (typically referred to as "returns")? The textbook answer is that prices reflect cash flows and discount rates. Cash flows are payments investors expect to realize from holding a given security—for example, the dividends that accrue to the equity holders over a company's lifetime. The discount rate (also known as the "cost of capital" or, as we will see in Chapter 5, "expected return" or "required return for the investor") is used to discount these future expected cash flows to today. It needs to reflect both the time value of money (translating dollar values in the future to dollars today) and the cash flows' riskiness (investors may not receive what they expect to receive). We will cover these fundamental drivers in this and the next section, and then we will introduce one more factor that matters for prices: investors' tastes.

To see why cash flows and discount rates are important, let's consider a very simplified security: if we buy that asset, we will get a certain payoff of $1,000 in exactly one year. (Yes, this example reflects a simple bond or perhaps a certificate of deposit.) How much money would you be willing to pay for such a security? Not more, and no less, than the value you will get in a year, discounted till today at the prevailing interest rate. Interest rates capture the time value of money, allowing you to translate dollars in the future into dollars today and vice versa. So, if the interest rate is 10%, then $1,000 you will receive a year from now is worth $909.09 in today's dollars (rounded to the nearest cent). You should be indifferent between buying and selling the security at that price. But if you were charged a higher price, say $950, you shouldn't pay it. You'd be better off depositing the $950 at a bank. In that case, after one year you'd collect more than $1,000: you'd get your initial investment of $950 back, plus the accrued interest of $95. All investors would (or at least should!) make this calculation, and no one would purchase the security at $950. At that point, supply and demand kick in. There is some supply of the security (presumably, someone is holding it and may be willing to sell it at $950), but there is no demand for the security at that price. The price must drop for supply and demand to meet and for the market to equilibrate.

Conversely, if you were quoted a price lower than $909.09, you should pounce on it. That deal is too good to be true. So good, in fact, that you would be willing to borrow at the 10% interest rate to buy as much of this security as possible. And you would not be alone—all investors would (or at least should) do likewise. The excess demand for the security would overwhelm its supply, and once more, prices would need to adjust. This time, the price would need to rise for demand and supply to meet.

You can also think about this a bit differently: if you buy this security at $909.09 and hold it for a year, you will realize a 10% return on your investment. If the price is higher ($950), then investing in the bond would net you a lower return (a bit more than 5%), which is obviously less attractive. In fact, it's less attractive than a bank deposit—instead of investing $950 in the security, you're better off putting it in the bank. What if the price is lower than $909.09, say $850? Well, in that case, the security is a steal. If you buy it at that price and hold it for a year, you'll earn close to 18%—much more attractive than the 10% the bank offers. As I said, you should pounce on this investment.

This simple example conveys a powerful intuition: the price of a security today depends on the cash flow we will get from that security (in our example, the promised $1,000) and the prevailing interest rates (in our example, 10%). This is all you need to know to figure out the "correct" price of securities with known and certain future payoffs. And when I say the price is "correct," I mean the price is not too high (such that it would earn you less return than a comparable investment) and not too low (such that it would earn you more return than you could otherwise).

Of course, most securities are more complex. First, there's risk: what happens in the future may diverge from our expectations. Second, we typically do not know the timing and the value of the cashflows the security may pay us in the future.

We will start with risk. It is convenient to think about it in terms of the discount rate we should use to translate the cashflows we expect to earn in the future into the price we're willing to pay for a security today. For example, a corporate bond may promise to pay $1,000 in a year, just as in our initial example. What is the correct price for this bond? Discounting the bond at the prevailing interest rate (say, 10%) gets you partial credit but leads to a biased answer. The 10% rate is appropriate for a guaranteed future payoff, as in our first example. However, a corporate bond's payoff is not quite certain—a firm may go bankrupt in the meantime. That's a risk, and it makes the corporate bond a relatively less attractive security. You wouldn't want to pay the whole $909.09 for the less attractive security— the price should be lower than $909.09. The interesting question is how much lower. We usually ask this question by referring to the discount rate rather than the price or, for bonds, to the yield we expect to earn on the bond should we hold it to maturity and should the bond deliver its promised payments. If the bond cost us $909.09, the yield would be equal to 10%. We know that this is too little, or, equivalently, that the price of the bond is too high. Instead, we need to increase the yield to reflect not only the time value (what the 10% does) but also the riskiness of the investment. Perhaps the corporation issuing the bond is a safe, blue-chip company that's very unlikely to go bankrupt in the near term. In such a case, the appropriate yield might be 12%. From the investor's point of view, 12% represents the reward for investing one's capital in this security for one year. This includes both the time value of money (the 10%) but also the credit premium (the 2%) that compensates investors for the risk they take on.

What happens when the firm issuing the corporate bond is riskier, or more likely to go bankrupt? Investors would demand more compensation. Perhaps now they require a yield of 20% to entice them to invest their capital in this bond. The bond would then trade at $833.33, which is just the $1,000 (the payoff if the firm does not go bankrupt), discounted at 20%. If the price changes to say $850, the yield on the bond would be below 20%, and no one would be interested in buying it. As before, the imbalance between demand and supply would push the price down until it reached $833.33. (A similar argument kicks in when the price drops below that amount.)

In general, we may address risks by referring not to yields but rather to expected returns (just as we saw in Chapter 2). The logic still applies. A stock's, or any other security's expected return will be a function of time value of money (the compensation we demand for tying our capital up in investing in this security) and the risk premium the security gives us. The risk premium generally captures those risks that actually matter to the investor. As we saw in the previous chapter, investors may be able to diversify away some of the risks of their allocation. But if you can avoid certain risks this easily, then you shouldn't expect to be compensated for them. In contrast, there are risks that are impossible to fully diversify, and these should involve some compensation for the investors who hold them. We will return to estimating expected returns in Chapter 4, when we discuss how ESG data may help us with that. We will also discuss some examples of ESG-type risks. There is much more to be learned about risk premia beyond the ESG aspects I mentioned. I will not expand on this topic here and will instead refer the interested reader to the textbook that I recommended in the last chapter.[1]

The second major difficulty that we need to address is that we typically do not know the timing and the value of a security's future cashflows. If you were to buy and hold a stock, you'd presumably do that because it entitles you to a piece of the underlying firm, and that firm will, over time, produce a stream of earnings and dividends. These can add up to a lot of value, but you simply do not know when in the future these cashflows may come, or how high they will be. This uncertainty presents a challenge in trying to figure out how much a company may fundamentally be worth and whether its price in the stock market may be too cheap or too expensive. This means that investors and analysts need to forecast future cashflows—perhaps the next earnings numbers the company will post, or perhaps estimate expected long-term growth in the company's earnings. We will see shortly how ESG information might help us with this task.

3.2   Efficient Markets?

Markets are said to be efficient when prices incorporate all relevant information about the underlying securities. The framework we've just introduced sheds light on what this statement actually means. We discussed the connection between cash flows, discount rates, and prices. The price is "right," in the efficient markets sense, when it is equal to the sum of the expected cashflows, discounted at the rate that reflects both the time value of money and the risk premium. That's a mouthful, so let's consider a few examples to illustrate the concept.

Suppose that a firm announces that it unexpectedly won a large contract. How should this affect the company's share price? Intuitively, the price should change—the market should price in all relevant information, and this information seems both relevant and new (it was unexpected). It also makes sense that the price should increase—winning a large contract is good news for the firm. But by how much specifically should the price go up? To answer the question, we would need to estimate the additional cash flows that the company will now be able to generate thanks to the new contract (we will assume that the news does not affect the riskiness of the firm). The discounted value of these additional cashflows tells us how much more the overall company should be worth, which in turn can be translated into an increase in the price per share.

For another example, let's say we are pricing a corporate bond, of the sort discussed earlier in this chapter. Suppose the issuing corporation is involved in a nasty lawsuit, and the range of potential damages is large enough that it might wipe out the company and not leave enough assets to pay for the outstanding bonds. In other words, the investors may not receive the payment the company originally promised. Now suppose that news breaks that the company settled the lawsuit out of court and that the settlement, while substantial, still leaves the company with a positive going concern. How would this news affect the price of the corporate bond? The cash flow of the bond does not change with this news: the company does not owe its bond investors any more, or any less, than it originally promised. But from the point of view of the bondholder, the company is now safer as it has warded off the risk of possibly ruinous litigation. The bondholders could reasonably expect the company to be more likely to pay off its obligation and thus will discount their (fixed) future cashflows at a lower rate. With less discounting, the present value of the cashflows is higher, which tells us how much more the bonds should now be worth.

Of course, in practice, it would be difficult for any one investor, or any one financial analyst, to come up with a precise estimate of the change in cash flows or the appropriate compensation of risk. Instead, we rely on the wisdom of crowds, or the actions of all market participants, to push the price toward the "right" level. Remarkably, the market seems to get this roughly right much of the time. To illustrate this, consider the catastrophe of the space shuttle Challenger.[2] This tragic event was followed by a lengthy investigation that eventually unearthed the specific component that malfunctioned during the space shuttle's launch. Amazingly, the stock market seems to have arrived at that conclusion in real time. The researchers studied the prices of the shuttle contractors and showed that the one that produced the faulty component stood out by experiencing abnormally high trading volume and falling the most in the hours immediately following the catastrophe. I know that this is a single case study or, if you prefer, an anecdote, but to me, it is also a testimony of how powerful the market is in aggregating and processing information.

So, most investors should probably assume that the market is quite efficient. At the very least, it is difficult to outguess the market and most investors have a poor track record doing so. To be sure, there are examples of the market making what seems like spectacular mistakes. There is even an academic paper that asked in its title "Can the market add and subtract?" and showed the evidence that the market may not always be able to do so.[3] In this book, we will also consider a range of potential inefficiencies that are related to ESG—for example, predicting returns using ESG-type information. But it is only prudent to approach such evidence cautiously. Identifying what information is incrementally relevant is one thing, and this book, and many similar books and whitepapers, can help investors with that task. But for serious investors, identifying such information is only the first step. They will then need to understand whether the information might already be priced in (if only because other investors also read relevant books and whitepapers). Then, the investor needs to design a risk-managed portfolio that reflects such information and finally trade that portfolio in a cost-effective manner. All of that is a formidable challenge. Many investors are well equipped to face it and to overcome it, but it is worth stressing that they typically have a thoughtful investment process that goes well beyond finding a signal to trade on.

Put differently, even if you find an interesting trading signal that may seem to contradict market efficiency, you still need to implement a portfolio around it. If the cost of building and trading the portfolio exceeds the benefit from the signal, then for all practical purposes you should probably treat the market as if it were efficient. There still may be a good reason to trade on the information in spite of the cost. Perhaps it might help you achieve your nonfinancial portfolio objectives, as we discussed in the previous chapter. You just shouldn't treat it as an "alpha signal" that helps you generate higher risk-adjusted performance.

3.3 Why Might ESG Information Matter for Prices?

Could ESG information help us predict future cashflows, or could it be useful for understanding security discount rates? If so, then ESG information will be relevant for today's prices—it will help us understand which securities should be relatively more expensive, and which securities should be cheaper.

For example, consider governance, or the "G" in ESG. A poorly governed firm may divert resources from projects that are in the best interest of shareholders, for example, by allowing the management team to engage in empire-building (growing the company beyond the scale that maximizes economic outcomes). Poor governance may also manifest itself in poor communication with stakeholders, not only because the firm may not have processes that generate precise information, but also because its corporate officers may try to obfuscate rather than inform. It is not a stretch to suggest that companies with poor governance may have lower prices because of relatively lower cash flows (since resources are diverted from their optimal uses), but perhaps also because of higher risk that increases the discount rate (since investors may require additional compensation to entice them to hold a poorly governed company's stock).

Governance is perhaps easiest to link to company fundamentals, but we could also suggest similar channels through which environmental or social information may be important for prices. For example, companies with poor carbon efficiency may need more natural resources to generate their output, emitting more greenhouse gasses for each widget they produce. Investors may expect that governments will impose a carbon tax (or, as we will see later in this book, may introduce carbon cap and trade schemes). This will increase the costs relatively more for heavy carbon emitters, eroding their cashflows. Moreover, the prospect of such regulation may be viewed as an additional risk by investors in the company, and these investors may again demand higher compensation for such risk, leading to higher discount rates and lower prices.

Similar examples abound for the social pillar of ESG. Firms that treat their employees poorly may not be able to hire the talent they need, or may need to deal with the costs and frictions of higher employee turnover. They might even be forced to pay relatively higher salaries to attract employees who normally would prefer to go elsewhere. All this may translate into lower productivity, lower margins, possibly higher incidence of workplace accidents, etc. These factors may be important determinants of stock or corporate bond prices.

Some readers will correctly observe that the examples I have chosen are positive for ESG, in that they suggest that an improvement in ESG characteristics will increase the economic value and hence a company's bond or share price. At this stage of our discussion, this is indeed just a conjecture. It is certainly possible that we might increase economic profits by going against ESG. For example, a company that emits toxic waste into the waterways may show lower costs because it avoids having to treat and neutralize harmful byproducts of its production. The cost savings might be large enough to more than offset the potential cost of fines or perhaps consumer backlash that the company may experience in the future. The good news is that it is probably easier to come up with the channels through which sustainability may benefit an underlying company (or country, etc.). As we will see later in this book, there's evidence that at least some such exposures correlate with positive outcomes for both fundamentals of the underlying business and share prices. In contrast, there doesn't seem to be much systematic evidence that companies acting against sustainability experience good economic outcomes, such as increases in profitability. There may even be some evidence (arguably somewhat mixed) that such businesses trade at discount to other firms, consistent with the idea that investors demand higher returns to compensate them for holding such companies. So, while it's not easy to prove a negative, we can probably cautiously conclude that there is little evidence to suggest that going against sustainability might improve business fundamentals or increase company prices.

In our discussion so far, I was careful to discuss how sustainability may influence prices *today*. This is an important qualifier. The fact that an ESG metric matters for (say) cash flows in the future does not automatically mean that they will also help us predict future prices. Recall our discussion of market efficiency—market prices should reflect all relevant information that is known to market participants. If we all agree that a company is well governed, environmentally efficient, and treats its employees well, then this information should be impounded into the company's share price today. In a perfectly efficient market, it should not be incrementally helpful in predicting where the share price may go in the future.

This may be a disappointing message for some sustainable investors, but I would stress the positive. The fact that markets correctly recognize the importance of ESG exposures and reflect it in asset prices is a welcome development. This aligns corporate incentives with sustainable investors' preferences. If the market prices sustainability in a timely manner, then companies that improve their ESG exposures (for example, their energy efficiency, or governance quality) can be rewarded with higher valuations and perhaps also lower cost of capital relatively soon afterward. In a perfectly efficient market, this would happen as soon as the news about the improvement is disclosed. In such a case, investors wouldn't be able to trade on this information.

If the market is not perfectly efficient, it may not reflect a firm's ESG characteristics immediately after their disclosure. In such cases, investors may have the best of both worlds: markets that reward sustainability and incentivize companies accordingly, and markets that do so slowly enough that it gives some investors an avenue to trade on ESG information and hope to earn risk-adjusted returns.

We can refine our thinking by going back to our discussion of the ESG-efficient frontier. When we introduced this concept in the last chapter, we discussed an ESG score that investors care about. Suppose that this score positively correlates with future cash flows. That is, firms with higher values of that score are expected to deliver higher cashflows than otherwise similar companies with lower ESG scores.

Now, let's suppose that the market is unaware of any ESG information or the relevance of such information for firm fundamentals. You are the only investor, or the only analyst, who has this insight. We already know from our first thought experiment that more information leads to better expected outcomes— especially if, as we assume here, the information is relevant for economic outcomes. This is great news, and you should be able to build a portfolio that will generate better risk-adjusted returns than the market overall.

How exactly do you go about that? If we compare two otherwise identical firms, one with a low ESG score and one with a high ESG score, we should expect that the latter will realize higher cash flows in the future. We also know that the market is unaware of this relationship, which means that other investors treat the future cashflows of the two firms as identical (remember, we assumed that the two companies are identical except for their sustainability profile). So, the market will price the companies incorrectly. The price of the high-ESG firm will be relatively too low since we know its expected cash flows are higher than what the market expects. The price of the low-ESG firm will be relatively too high, because its expected cashflows are weaker than what the market assumes. If you've ever heard the cliché that investors should "buy low and sell high," then you know what to do here. Buy the high-ESG firm at a price that's too low, and sell the low-ESG firm at a price that's too high. (As an aside, it is prudent to remind ourselves that this "ESG trade" is likely only one ingredient of the overall portfolio. A savvy investor will likely want to take advantage of other [non-ESG] patterns in expected returns, diversify risks, etc.)

You expect to earn a nice return on your trade, and let's now turn to the question when this return may be realized. The timing depends on how quickly the market appreciates the difference in company cash flows. In principle, it might happen only when the cash flows are actually paid. But, with luck, you might see the benefits earlier, for example, after analysts eventually revise their earnings estimates. Or, as we will see in a moment, your extra return may also materialize when the market overall starts to understand the importance of ESG information.

Figure 3.1 is a stylized illustration of this mechanism. It plots expected returns on a given stock (or a portfolio of stocks) as a function of the ESG score. In the "ESG-unaware investors" case that we have just discussed, the higher the score, the higher expected future cash flows and, since the market does not appreciate this fact, the higher the future investment returns.

It would probably be naïve to hope that you can preserve your investment edge: over time, other investors, analysts, academic researchers, etc., will notice the relationship between ESG and future cash flows (or, perhaps more likely, between ESG and future returns). Eventually investors will start incorporating this information in their portfolios. Prices will then adjust based on a simple

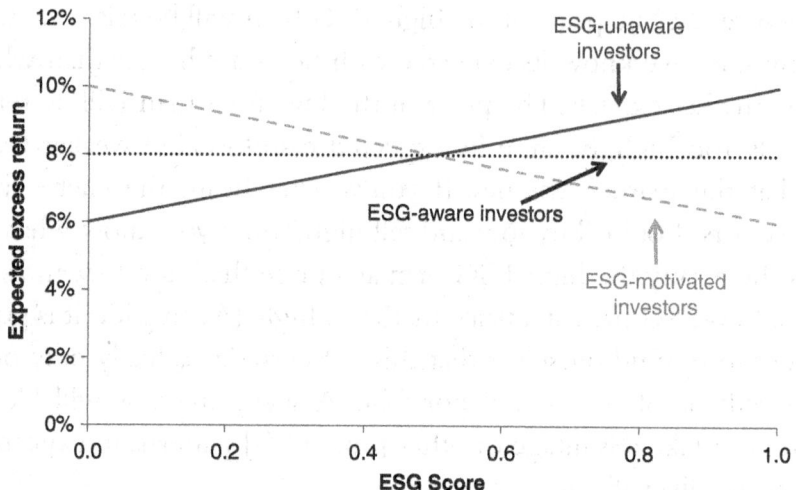

Figure 3.1 ESG and expected returns. The chart plots expected returns as a function of ESG, across different market environments, assuming that higher ESG scores predict higher future cash flows.

Source: Pedersen, L., Fitzgibbons, S., and Pomorski, L. (2021). Responsible investing: the ESG-efficient frontier. *Journal of Financial Economics*, 142 (2): 572–597.

supply and demand argument. Eventually, the market starts to understand the importance of ESG information, and many others will adopt the same positioning you did: investors will demand more of the high-ESG stock, driving its price higher, and will try to sell the low-ESG stock, driving its price lower. Equilibrium will be reached when, as you probably guessed, the prevailing prices correctly reflect the difference in the expected cash flows of the two companies.

At this point, the high-ESG firm is still superior in terms of its future cash flows, but it is now also more expensive. Investors who buy this firm are buying the higher cash flow at a higher price, contending with a lower expected return than you originally earned. On the flip side, the poor-ESG firm is now cheaper. If you buy it, you will get the lower cashflow at a cheaper price than before, making it more attractive. Since we assumed that the two firms are identical except for their ESG scores, it stands to reason that their expected returns are now equal. Figure 3.1 illustrates this under the "ESG aware investors" scenario: in a perfectly efficient market, information about ESG affecting fundamentals will be fully incorporated into the price. Prices of high-ESG stocks are now higher, and investors won't be able to generate risk-adjusted returns trading on ESG information.

This ESG repricing occurs as we move from an ESG-unaware to ESG-aware environment. A key feature of this repricing is the opposite movement in prices and in expected future returns. As we saw, when the market learns that ESG is important for future fundamentals, prices of high-ESG firms increase—but the future expected returns on such firms decrease. At the same time, the market reprices poor ESG firms as well: their price drops to account for the now-obvious lower expected cashflows and, since you can now buy these cashflows at a lower price, the poor-ESG stock's expected return is now higher than it used to be.

This repricing is good news to those investors who—like you—positioned themselves on ESG before the broader market adjusts. The high-ESG companies you bought are appreciating, while the poor-ESG firms you sold are dropping in price. As I alluded to earlier, this is one way how your informational advantage pays off in higher risk-adjusted returns. However, in this case, once the market adjusts, your advantage disappears. From then on, trading on ESG information does not change your expected returns because the market correctly reflects it in the prevailing prices.

3.4 Investor Preference for ESG and the Resulting Sin Premium

Figure 3.1 has one last line that we haven't discussed yet: the scenario of ESG-motivated investors. We know such investors from our earlier thought experiments. They seek not only high financial returns, but they also incorporate additional ESG goals and preferences in their portfolios.

As we move from the "ESG-aware" to the "ESG-motivated" case, investors keep on buying high-ESG firms and keep on selling poor-ESG companies. They do so beyond what the fundamentals say. A high-ESG company will be bid up to a price even higher than could be justified by its cash flows; a poor-ESG firm will be sold off to a price cheaper than its cash flows would suggest. Importantly, the investors who do so are not making a mistake. They correctly form their portfolios by shifting them even more toward high-ESG companies. This is because these companies are now even more valuable in that they play an additional role in investors' portfolios. So, not surprisingly, investors are willing to pay a relatively higher price for them. Put differently, investors are willing to accept a lower rate of expected return going forward because they now get some additional benefit from some stocks. A similar argument holds for poor-ESG stocks. Investors are no longer comfortable with the "ESG-aware" level of prices, because these stocks now conflict with investors' ESG portfolio goals. To entice investors to hold these stocks (and for the markets to clear), the price needs to drop even further. Put differently, investors now demand even higher expected returns for holding these stocks as compensation for reducing their overall portfolios' ESG score.

If enough investors in the market exhibit such an ESG preference, the relationship between ESG scores and future returns will flip, as shown in Figure 3.1. We will arrive at a seemingly paradoxical case where higher ESG scores correlate not only with higher cash flows but also with lower future returns. This phenomenon is usually referred to as a "sin premium," because it implies that when investors are willing to pay extra for ESG, then holding anti-ESG (so, "sin") portfolios leads to higher expected returns. Importantly, these higher returns are not a compensation for risk or for poorer quality of future cashflows, but rather a direct consequence of investors' tastes and preferences.[4] If you find yourself in an ESG-motivated market and you are one of the few investors who do not have any ESG preferences, then you should be interested in buying low-ESG and selling high-ESG stocks. Doing so will help you earn a higher expected return. You may need to hold assets with horrible ESG characteristics, but you should not mind since you have no view, positive or negative, on sustainability.

At this point, we are ready to move from our thought experiments to the real world and apply our newly gained economic intuition to actual markets. We will start by looking for evidence of a sin premium. We are most likely to find it where we identify a clear "sin" exposure that sustainable investors broadly agree on, and that they can readily identify in their portfolios. If you polled investors about what they consider "sin," the most popular answers would include tobacco, controversial weapons, and fossil fuels (and perhaps climate change more broadly—we will discuss it in much more detail later in this book).

For our first foray into the data, we will start with tobacco. Restricting exposure to that industry has been one of the longest-standing and perhaps the most popular sustainability-related portfolio objectives. This is one of the few aspects of sustainability where investors agree on definitions: there is relatively little uncertainty about which companies produce tobacco products, or even distribute or market such products. There is also a broad agreement on how to define the nonfinancial portfolio objective: the goal is simply to avoid any exposure to issuers with any meaningful revenue from tobacco (say, more than 5% or 10% of a firm's overall revenue). Tobacco-averse investors never purchase such securities; if tobacco appears in their portfolios anyway (e.g., if an existing portfolio company acquires a tobacco producer), then they sell the implicated securities.

The agreement on the definition and the straightforward implementation makes tobacco an ideal laboratory to study a potential sin premium. The more tobacco-averse investors there are in the market, the lower the demand for tobacco-related securities. Eventually, prices adjust and tobacco becomes cheaper, not because of some fundamental news about the underlying businesses but because of investor tastes. Investors who are willing to purchase tobacco at these lower prices stand to gain relatively higher expected return than they would have otherwise.

At least, that's the theory. Do we see any evidence of this behavior in the market? Let's check, using data provided as a public service on Professor Ken French's website.[5] The website is easily accessible for readers who may want to replicate or even extend the analysis I'm discussing here. Specifically, we will look at returns to overall industries, dividing the overall market into 30 industry segments, one of which is "Tobacco and tobacco products."

We learned from the previous chapter that the Sharpe ratio is a convenient way to summarize the risk and return of an investment portfolio. We can use that insight to describe the risk and return of the tobacco industry. If there is a sin premium, then we should see a relatively high Sharpe ratio. To assess the relative magnitude, we will compare it to the Sharpe ratio of a few other selected industries, as well to the median industry and to the overall market. Figure 3.2 shows the results of this analysis.

Tobacco's Sharpe ratio, at 0.51, is higher than that of any other industry, and noticeably higher than the market's overall 0.43. This is consistent with a sin premium for the tobacco industry. However, it may give us a pause that a few other plausible "sin" industries do not stand out quite as much. For example, the alcohol industry ("Beer & Liquor") has a Sharpe ratio that is roughly similar to that of the overall market and lower than, say, the

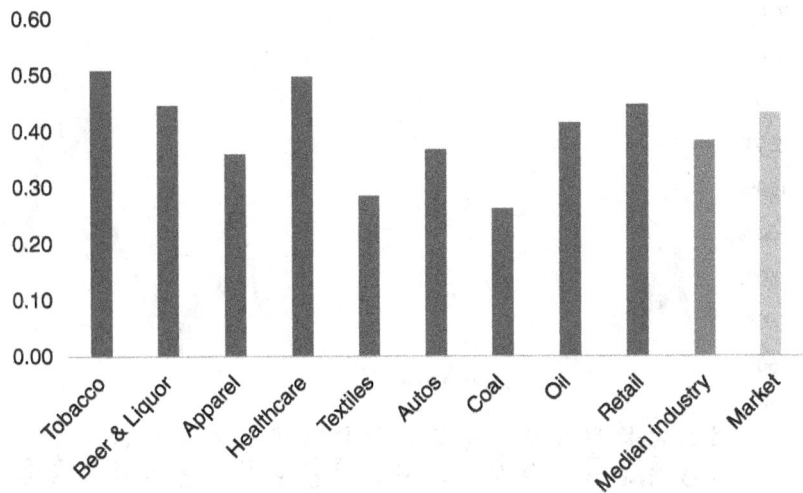

Figure 3.2 Sharpe ratios of selected industries, the median industry, and the market overall.

Source: Ken French's data library.

Healthcare or Retail industries. Another industry ESG investors may avoid, Coal, has a clearly lower Sharpe ratio that the median industry does. We may be able to explain this. Perhaps tobacco is a much longer-standing restriction, and the market has had plenty of time to transition to "ESG motivated." In contrast, perhaps coal is a much more recent development and the market is only now repricing this industry. We saw earlier in this chapter that when the repricing happens, the prices of poor-ESG securities drop. These securities do have higher expected returns going forward, but perhaps we can only measure these over long periods following the repricing—and maybe simply too little time has passed for us to see this with oil and coal. Perhaps—this is certainly a possibility, but not something we can substantiate with the data we have on hand.

Another analysis we can undertake is comparing how tobacco fared over time to what the overall market did. This is what

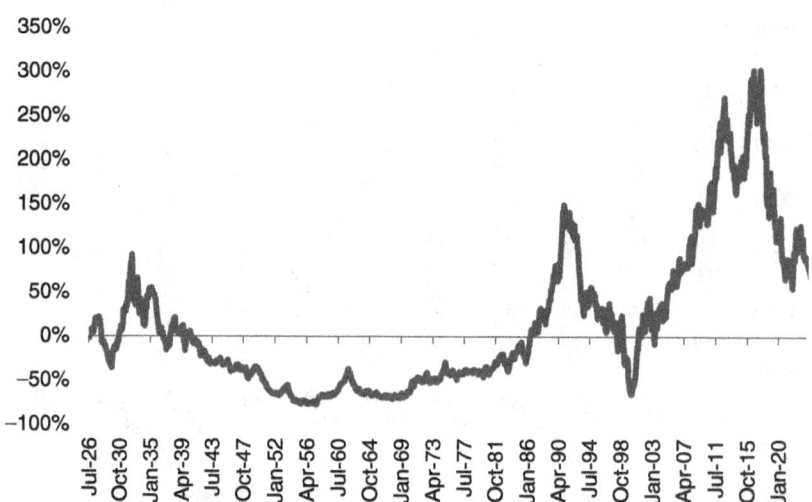

Figure 3.3 Cumulative difference in returns between the tobacco industry and the overall market.

Source: Ken French's data library.

Figure 3.3 does. The figure plots the cumulative difference in returns between the two, starting from zero at the beginning of our sample in July 1926.

Consistent with the higher Sharpe ratio of tobacco, the industry generated a cumulative difference of about 88% versus the market. That's not a bad return to earn over close to a century, but earning it clearly was not a smooth ride. Tobacco was at times meaningfully lower than the overall market, trailing it by about 75% of cumulative return in the 1950s and 1960s. At other times, it handily beat it, delivering three times higher cumulative returns around 2017. If you were unlucky enough to invest in tobacco around that peak, though, then over the subsequent six years, you would have trailed the market by a whopping 200%. So, even if there is a sin premium, earning it may not be an easy investment experience.

Before we move on, let me offer one last point on this topic. Suppose you cover the right-hand side of Figure 3.3 and stop the chart in 2017. This is the peak of tobacco's outperformance over the broader market. If you were conducting your analysis at that point in time, arguably, you'd be more likely to conclude that there is a sin premium than you would at any other time in this sample. Surprisingly, according to a research paper published around that time, it turns out that even in this situation, the sin premium is not as obvious as it may seem.[6] The researchers pointed out that tobacco stocks tend to be relatively profitable and more defensive (less cyclical) than other stocks. This may not be too surprising, given the nature of the industry's product: people who smoke may be less price-sensitive, and they continue to smoke in both economic expansions and depressions. At the same time, we know from earlier research that stocks that are profitable and defensive deliver higher average returns. The researchers asked whether the good performance of tobacco might be due to those other characteristics, and not necessarily because of a sin premium. And indeed, once they controlled for profitability and defensiveness, the sin premium disappeared.

My own stance is that sin premia are real—it is difficult to argue with the basic supply and demand argument we have built in this section. At the same time, they can be frustratingly difficult to detect in the data. As we just saw, there are doubts even for tobacco, which seems to be our best shot for a sin premium. In my view, this is both because tobacco-free investors are still a minority, but also because the markets are very liquid and it is generally easy to find a counterparty who is willing to take the other side of your trade. In other words, for all sustainable investors who want to sell tobacco, there is a healthy competition among the remaining investors that stops the price from dropping too low.

Notes

1. Bodie, Z., Kane, A., and Marcus, A.J. (2013). *Essentials of Investments*, 13e. McGraw Hill.
2. See Maloney, M.T. and Mulherin, J.H. (2003). The complexity of price discovery in an efficient market: the stock market reaction to the Challenger crash. *Journal of Corporate Finance*, 9 (4): 453–479.
3. Lamont, O.A. and Thaler, R.H. (2003). Can the market add and subtract? Mispricing in tech stock carve-outs. *Journal of Political Economy*, 111 (2): 227–268.
4. It is a relatively novel idea that what matters for stock prices is not just risk and return, but also investor tastes and preferences. However, this idea is well established in both theoretical and empirical academic literature. See for example Fama, E.F. and French, K.R. (2007). Disagreement, tastes, and asset prices. *Journal of Financial Economics*, 83 (3): 667–689.
5. https://mba.tuck.dartmouth.edu/pages/faculty/ken.french/data_library.html
6. Blitz, D. and Fabozzi, F. (2017). Sin stocks revisited: resolving the sin stock anomaly. *Journal of Portfolio Management*, 44 (1): 105–111.

Chapter 4

Can ESG Even Be Measured?

So far, we discussed ESG at a very high level, simply referring to some abstract "ESG score." This is fine for theory, but to put theory into practice, we need to define what such an ESG score might be and how it could be measured. We now take on this task.

In our discussion, we will take the perspective of a portfolio manager who builds a portfolio of assets (say, stocks). We may want to use ESG data to seek out attractive investment opportunities and increase the return of the portfolio, reduce its risk, or ideally achieve both of these financial goals. You will recognize this as "ESG integration," which we discussed in Chapter 2. But we will also ask how we may be able to use ESG data to achieve social or environmental goals for the portfolio. To do this, we will still aim to generate a maximally attractive risk–return profile but do so while keeping the portfolio's ESG characteristics above some minimal threshold.

To achieve these various goals, portfolio managers need to interrogate ESG data from various perspectives. Most importantly, they need to decide whether the data actually measures what it claims it does. For example, how do we know that ESG ratings really capture ESG? As we will see, this part of due diligence may be difficult and quite frustrating. Because of that, some investors choose to forgo this important step and just assume that the data is good enough simply because it comes from a reputable provider. I believe we can do better, and I will outline at least some intuitive tests that investors, or the interested public, may undertake and hopefully increase their confidence in ESG data. Moreover, we will see that we can avoid much of the complication, and perhaps frustration, if instead of asking the broad question about "ESG," we first narrow it down to a specific dimension of ESG that the investor may care about the most (e.g., carbon emissions, diversity of the workforce).

For ESG integration, we will also need to test whether the data might be a useful predictor for returns, or for risks of the underlying assets. Perhaps surprisingly, this tends to be a relatively easier task. In principle, all you need is a sample of stocks (or some other assets), data that measures the ESG characteristics of these stocks, and the stocks' returns. In fact, this is exactly what we did at the end of the last chapter. We started with industries (each of which is a collection of stocks), and a very simple ESG indicator, labeling the stocks in the Tobacco industry as "not ESG-aligned" and labeling all other industries as "ESG-aligned." We then looked at subsequent returns, as a function of ESG alignment. Using the same data, you could also try to analyze the variability of returns, again as a function of ESG. This is an easy template to follow, so, not surprisingly, there have been literally thousands of research papers trying to correlate ESG and returns (many fewer papers look at ESG and risk, but this category is also quite plentiful).[1] We will discuss a few of these studies in more detail, highlighting those that have been early and more impactful, but also those that are particularly careful in how they establish the effect (or lack of an effect). I will also stress the key question of how to convince yourself that the results, established for one specific historical sample, may still be useful going forward. Finding a correlation with historical returns is merely the first step, and should be followed with additional analyses. This is particularly important because ESG data often has short historical samples, and any analyses are made challenging by potential market transitions and repricing effects of the sort we discussed in Chapter 3. This may sometimes leave room for interpretation and may lead to very different investment beliefs, as we will see when we discuss the interplay between carbon emissions and returns.

Finally, we will go over a small case study based on one of my papers. I will explain how we identified an investor need for a specific climate measurement, how we approached broadly available data to see if they might satisfy that need, and finally, how we developed a new climate measure and empirically validated its usefulness.

4.1   ESG ratings

Perhaps the most obvious way to measure the ESG characteristics of a firm (and perhaps also of a country, municipality, etc.) is to ask an expert who specializes in this task. There are multiple external data vendors who can play this role. The two that are arguably the most influential are MSCI (whose essential product in this space is the suite of MSCI ESG Ratings) and Sustainalytics (owned by Morningstar and whose main product is ESG Risk Ratings). Still, there are scores of other providers, offering both broad ESG measures and narrower metrics of specific issues that investors care about, some of which we will discuss later.

ESG ratings are widely used, with survey evidence suggesting that more than half of institutional investors use this data in their investment process, and some surveys reporting that 90% of investors either currently use ESG ratings or expect to do so in the future.[2] The ratings are also widely discussed and often criticized. We will go over some common concerns and misperceptions in this section. I will also discuss how investors may use such rankings. While I will stop short of dissecting any one specific provider, I will explain what I believe is a good way to think about this data more generally.

The first question we need to address is what ESG ratings actually measure. If you consult their documentation, you will frequently see terms such as "ESG quality" or "ESG risk," although it is rarely clarified what these terms mean. This can easily lead to confusion because, as I have stressed in the introduction to this book, there is no common definition of ESG that all investors share. We likely agree on broad concepts, but we all have different views of what specific issues may be important, how to measure such issues, or how to weigh them one against the other. Not surprisingly, the same is true for ESG rating companies. This leads to meaningful differences between what different providers' scores capture and, not surprisingly, relatively low correlations between their measures. We will come back to this thorny question in a moment.

Moreover, the investor needs to decide what it is they want to do with ESG ratings. To some extent, the data providers can help through a description of their data. Most providers highlight risk, arguing that their ratings capture important exposures that may harm a firm's business. For example, a firm with very poor Social characteristics may lose customer loyalty, may find it difficult to attract new talented employees, etc. A minority of data providers also explicitly focuses on valuation and suggests that their ratings may help investors predict future stock returns. This may be because, according to the data provider, we may be in an ESG-unaware environment of the type we considered in the previous chapter. For example, if the market underappreciates the link between certain ESG characteristics and future profitability, and if the data provider is skilled at identifying such characteristics, then their scores may indeed predict returns. That's a lot of ifs, so you will not be surprised that the evidence that broad ESG scores predict returns is patchy—more on this later. Finally, an important use case of the data is identifying which companies are more acceptable for sustainability-minded investors and reporting this information to various stakeholders.

We will review all these scenarios, but no matter the use case, investors should carry out at least some basic due diligence to ensure that the ESG rating they consider is suitable for their needs.

Unfortunately, this due diligence is often lacking, or at best is limited to ensuring the data comes from a reputable provider.

My recommendation is not to skimp on due diligence, even if this means you may need to devote more resources to the data even before you use it in a portfolio. At a minimum, you want to understand a provider's methodology and the recommended uses for the data. Ideally, you would also subject the data to a battery of your own tests, reflecting your needs and expectations. We already alluded to some basic tests of return predictability, but you will see a number of additional tests later in this chapter. These will help you understand the data better, ideally to the point that you can use your analyses to defend using that data in live portfolios.

Finally, another part of your due diligence may be reviewing published research that uses that particular dataset. One of the consequences of the widespread interest in ESG investing is the deluge of papers that study various ESG ratings or other related variables. Most of these studies are interested exclusively in return predictability, but there are also papers dealing with risk, impact (more on this in the next chapter), etc. Investors and even professional researchers can be easily overwhelmed by the sheer volume of such studies. Moreover, as you might expect, the key findings and claims may differ dramatically from study to study. Fortunately, there are some high-level guidelines that may help us here. As with any research, your task will be easier if you prioritize those authors that you deem more reputable and err on the side of research published in peer-reviewed journals. You could also let the market identify the most important papers and focus on those that attract the most subsequent citations or that are the most read and downloaded. I realize that these last pieces of advice sound elitist, but for better or worse, the reputation of the journal and the number of citations are likely the best measures of the quality of published research (not ideal, just the best we have).

Sounds daunting, doesn't it? I guess that's one of the reasons why you may prefer to read a book like this one, where the author adhered to the above process, parsed the requisite papers, and is willing to distill the findings for you. The usual caveat applies, though: the conclusions are mine and, to some extent, might reflect my tastes. For example, some of the papers in this field are my own. Having said that, here are what I consider the main stylized facts that emerge from such analyses.

4.1.1   Predicting returns using ESG ratings

As I mentioned, the most frequent question addressed in research papers is whether ESG ratings predict future returns. Based on my reading of the literature and on my own research, the answer is "not really." Yes, across the thousands of studies I mentioned earlier you can find many that claim return predictability. However, if you focus on papers published in top-tier academic journals, or those that subsequently attract the most citations, this is simply not the case anymore. Moreover, I put a lot of weight on whether the findings generalize. I am rarely swayed by a seemingly strong result that only appears in one historical sample, one specific market, using one specific piece of ESG data. I will trust the evidence much more if the results hold across different samples, if it can be replicated by other researchers, etc. This is a high bar to clear for research on ESG ratings (although later in this chapter we will see research on specific sub-dimensions of ESG that does clear this bar). It is much easier to point to systematic studies that show no evidence of predictability. As I was finishing the first draft of this book, I came across a new paper that analyzed thousands of stocks traded in 48 different countries and assessed ESG ratings from seven different providers. The bottom line is that the authors found *"very little evidence that ESG ratings are related to global stock returns."*[3]

My skepticism is reinforced by the realized performance of sustainable stock indexes that are based on ESG ratings. Such indexes are rules-based investment strategies developed to give investors broad market exposure, while emphasizing (or holding exclusively) stocks that rank well on a provider's ESG scorecard. A recent paper considered such sustainable indexes and compared their hypothetical performance before they were officially incepted, to the returns realized after the indexes went live.[4] The indexes considered come from different providers and leveraged different ESG ratings. Nonetheless, in all cases, the live results were disappointing. For two of the indexes, the researchers had access to pre-launch historical simulations. Perhaps not surprisingly, the simulations showed outperformance of the sustainable indexes versus the regular (non-ESG-labeled) index covering the same market. However, in the years after launch, one of the sustainability indexes delivered about neutral performance compared to the regular, non-ESG index, while the second sustainable index noticeably underperformed. For the third index the study considered, the authors did not have historical simulations, but documented that over its live history, the index did not deliver meaningfully different performance than its non-ESG version.

You may be disappointed by this negative result. I understand, and this is certainly no evidence that ESG ratings might allow you to beat the market. But if you consider this from another angle, I would say that achieving performance roughly in line with a regular index is actually fantastic news. The indexes in question were meaningfully narrower than the broad market index, focusing on as little as 50% and in one case only 10% of the underlying market. Presumably, the stocks included in these indexes had good enough ESG characteristics to appeal to even the most stringent sustainable investor. If such an investor could still match the overall market performance with so few stocks, then the financial penalty one incurs for achieving a meaningful improvement in ESG may, in fact, be remarkably low. In other words, these sustainable indexes may still be on the flat part of the ESG efficient frontier, where meaningful improvements in sustainability only carry a very mild penalty to purely financial performance.

Finally, I would argue that the potential link between ESG ratings and subsequent returns is doubtful from first-principles reasoning. Think back to our discussion of market efficiency. The market is constantly processing new information, and many investors compete fiercely to be the first to impound it into prices and earn extra returns while doing so. And in the case of ESG ratings, you don't even need to work very hard to get the data, since many leading providers post their ratings on public websites.[5] To beat the market, you may need to work a bit harder and find less obvious indicators of sustainability. We will review some illustrative examples shortly.

4.1.2 Predicting risk using ESG ratings

There is more to the claim that ESG ratings may provide insights about the risk of the underlying companies. At least, there is a clear correlation between such ratings and a variety of risk measures. My co-authors and I documented that this holds for both statistical measures coming from a risk model (for example, volatility or beta) but also for measures of the fundamental risk of the underlying business (for example, credit risk or the variability of the earnings the company generates).[6] These relationships are quite strong empirically. For example, when we compared the stocks in the best ESG quintile (20% of stocks with the highest ESG ratings) with the stocks in the worst ESG quintile, the latter had volatilities that were 15% higher than the former. This is good news, at least for investors who may have few other tools to measure and manage risk, or those who trade their portfolios very infrequently. I say this because we also showed that knowing the ESG rating of a stock today can help you predict how risky this stock will be next year, or even five years down the line. This insight holds even if you control for a variety of the stock's statistical and fundamental risk measures. This means that if you build a portfolio today and tilt it toward stocks with strong ESG ratings, and revisit this portfolio a year from now, I would predict that it will hold relatively safer stocks than those in an otherwise similar portfolio that instead tilted toward poor ESG ratings. This is an interesting finding, but, in practice, many investors trade more frequently, perhaps once every few weeks or months. At such shorter horizons, the purely statistical risk model catches up to news relatively quickly, and the incremental value of ESG ratings is not as large. It's not to say that ESG is useless—but the additional insights it yields about the next few weeks are similar to what you would learn from other, non-ESG sources of information.

But this nuance about long- versus short-term prediction may actually be a moot point. At least some leading providers of statistical risk models have recently started to enrich them with ESG ratings data. For example, MSCI's Barra risk models *"integrate [a] sustainability factor to understand new and emerging risks and their impact on portfolio performance."*[7] This means that investors using these models will implicitly rely on ESG scores anyway. These may only marginally influence the risk model's prediction over the short horizon, but they are an increasingly accepted part of investors' toolboxes.

4.1.3 Using ESG ratings to build ESG-labeled strategies

Besides returns and risk, a key usage of ESG ratings is identifying issuers that may not belong in an ESG-labeled portfolio or, conversely, those issuers that are particularly attractive in such strategies. For example, ratings may help identify portfolio companies that have externalities that affect society or the environment, and a portfolio manager may want to emphasize firms with positive externalities (through a process referred to as positive screening) and exclude the ones with negative externalities (restrictions, or negative screening).

This use case is important even if ESG ratings correlate with neither the expected returns nor the risk of the underlying firm. This is because in this case, ESG ratings address investors' non-financial needs. This may be relevant not only for investors who have a natural preference for good-citizen companies but perhaps also for investors who are averse to the headline risk of their portfolio companies. ESG data might help such investors avoid companies with, say, negative media coverage, either because the data provider can identify such companies before the media coverage starts or (more realistically) because they downgrade them promptly once such coverage occurs.

As with risk or returns, this use case also requires due diligence of the data. However, unlike risk and returns, we can no longer rely on readily accessible observations of how well a stock did or how much risk it experienced. We rarely observe a direct manifestation of a company's ESG-ness; if we did, I guess we wouldn't need ESG ratings in the first place. So, to test such metrics, we may need to look for proxies of what good or bad ESG characteristics look like. We could check how the data behaves around some obvious ESG events in the past. For example, suppose a whistleblower reveals that a company knew its products were toxic but hid that fact from the public. We could then expect an ESG rating to show indications of poor Social (harm to customers) and Governance (hiding bad news) characteristics for this company. Ideally, such indications would be apparent even before the event in question happens, as you'd expect if ESG ratings could predict ESG controversies. In practice, this would raise the bar too high because predicting controversies is extremely challenging. However, we could insist that, at the minimum, the data reflects major ESG controversies in a timely fashion—in our example, that S and G scores for the company drop soon after the whistleblower goes public. If the scores do not change, the investor should probably discuss this with the data provider—there may be legitimate reasons, and understanding them may increase the investor's comfort with the data.

Lastly, for this investment use case, there are clear benefits to relying on a third-party ESG rating provider. This assures a common language for the investment community and comparability across different strategies and different managers. You need such comparability and external verification to ensure that the portfolio is indeed what is advertised (e.g., holding stocks commonly thought to be sustainable) but also for the more prosaic, but still very important, reporting purposes. In contrast, if a manager reports that a strategy scores well on that manager's proprietary ESG score, the usefulness of this information is limited because the investor may not be able to compare the manager to his or her other mandates. Finally, it is often beneficial to have a third-party opinion that may provide an unbiased opinion about the ESG bona fides of a portfolio.

Of course, the fact that ESG ratings come from a third party is less relevant for return or risk prediction. If the data works, the investor should be, in principle, indifferent as to where the data comes from. Conversely, data that comes from a third party that many stakeholders trust can be worthwhile for one's portfolio process even if it does not reliably predict risk or return—you'd just use it for non-risk, non-return reasons.

4.1.4 (Lack of) correlation across providers

One of the common complaints about ESG ratings is that the data is lowly correlated across providers. For a while, it was popular for the media to report examples of companies with dramatically different scores from different ESG data providers. For example, *The Wall Street Journal* asked in the title of a September 17, 2018 article "Is Tesla or Exxon more sustainable? It depends whom you ask." The article proceeded to compare Tesla scores across three ESG data providers, FTSE, Sustainalytics, and MSCI. The three disagreed, often spectacularly. For example, when assessing the Environmental pillar of ESG, FTSE ranked Tesla as worst in class, Sustainalytics gave is a relatively neutral score, and MSCI ranked it as best in class. In contrast, all three providers were in relative agreement about Exxon, giving it roughly median scores on Environment.

It is easy to understand why such examples are troubling to investors interested in ESG data. If even the experts are at a loss about a well-known stock such as Tesla, then perhaps any exercise in measuring ESG is ultimately futile. Fortunately, the Tesla predicament seems to be an exception, not the rule. When we systematically compare ESG ratings across stocks and across providers, they are actually positively correlated. Based on the analysis in one of the most cited articles on this issue, if we were to randomly select two ESG data providers, the correlation between their ESG scores would be 0.54.[8] (A correlation of 1 would mean that the scores move in perfect unison; 0 indicates no relationship; and -1 implies perfect divergent, similar to what we saw in the Tesla case above.) So, ESG ratings actually correlate positively across providers. This means that when a stock ranks above average according to one provider, it also tends to be above average according to the other.

This positive correlation suggests that there is some commonality in how data providers view the ESG-ness of the firms they cover. But perhaps the correlation is not high enough. A frequent complaint is that 0.54 is paltry when we compare it to correlations in credit ratings, which are much closer to the perfect 1. But, in my view, this simply is not a relevant comparison. Credit ratings have a very specific purpose: to predict whether a company will be able to repay its debt. Companies that are unable to do so are in default, which is a well-defined event that credit rating agencies can observe and then model. In contrast, ESG rating agencies are trying to summarize a company's multifaceted sustainability profile, which is much more subjective than a credit event can be. I would argue this makes credit ratings and ESG ratings conceptually different, and it is not obvious at all that they should exhibit the same patterns in correlations.

If we need to compare ESG ratings to a different quantity, it would be more reasonable to contrast them with earnings forecasts that sell-side analysts provide to their clients. Even here, the comparison is imperfect. Earnings forecasts, much like credit events, can be directly compared against a concrete corporate event—something that cannot be said about ESG ratings. On the other hand, while there are only three leading credit rating agencies, there are many more sell-side analysts who are prepared to forecast company earnings—just like ESG rating providers, which are similarly fragmented (by some counts, there are over a hundred of them, although we also see a lot of consolidation in this industry). Moreover, while credit ratings are indeed highly correlated across the three leading providers, earnings forecasts can vary a lot across analysts. In fact, there is a voluminous academic literature that discusses analyst forecast dispersion and how it may correlate with future returns and other economic quantities.[9] I haven't heard many complaints that different analysts may have different forecasts of a company's earnings. If anything, there may be value in some analysts being able to bring a new perspective and stand out from the crowd. I would use the same standard when it comes to providers of ESG ratings.

Finally, we can also try to explain the seemingly low correlation of ESG ratings if we look at the data providers using the tools of industrial organization. Data providers are companies, and when they enter a market, they presumably do so based on their economic analysis and in the hope of generating profits. Put yourself in the position of a new data provider who wants to sell ESG ratings. How would you structure your business? Would you try to focus on the exact same dimensions as an existing provider, and perhaps try to assess them with more precision? Or could you come up with a differentiated view of which dimensions of ESG are more important, perhaps coupled with different data sources you'd use? I would argue that the latter approach may be more attractive. It may allow you to customize your data for investors with specific needs that are not yet served by existing providers. You will also be able to differentiate your data product for other investors, and maybe even earn higher margins than you would producing a very similar commodity to what other providers do. So, perhaps the positive-but-not-perfect correlations are actually an economic decision of the data provider firms, and not an accident or a testimony to the inability to measure ESG characteristics.

4.2   Disaggregated ESG data

So far, we have discussed ESG ratings, which attempt to summarize all ESG issues in a single number or label. As I mentioned at the beginning of this chapter, such ratings are perhaps the most obvious piece of ESG data that investors start with. Over time, as they get more experience, investors increasingly focus on specific dimensions of ESG that they care about and seek differentiated data that capture such dimensions. It turns out that once we zero in on such individual ESG issues, many of the problems of aggregate ESG ratings go away. Moreover, at this more granular level, we may see much more robust evidence of ESG data predicting returns or other economic quantities.

We will now go over examples of such granular E, S, and G measures. These examples are not exhaustive. I picked them because the evidence behind them is, in my view, relatively strong (if only because most of these ideas have been replicated by at least one other research team), but also because I thought they were good examples of creative measurement of soft information, for example, how well a company treats its employees. In most cases, I will focus on using a given measure to predict future stock returns, acknowledging that, as we have learned, this is not the only reason why investors care about ESG data.

Across the examples we will analyze, most will show a positive correlation with subsequent returns. That is, we will see evidence that more attractive ESG characteristics are rewarded with higher subsequent returns. This is not a selection bias on my part. There are surprisingly few studies that document a negative correlation; those few that do, typically discuss a sin premium of the sort we've already encountered in Chapter 3 (and will discuss once more in Section 4.2.3).

To interpret the positive correlation between various granular ESG metrics and subsequent returns, we will leverage the groundwork we built in the previous chapter. I will argue that the patterns in returns are consistent with an ESG-unaware market: a market inefficiency, in which most investors underappreciate the relationship between ESG characteristics and the firm's fundamentals. Other explanations are less likely. For example, the return patterns are inconsistent with a risk story. For such an explanation to hold, we would need to argue that stocks with attractive ESG characteristics (e.g., stronger corporate governance) are riskier than other stocks. That seems implausible. At the same time, if we agree on the inefficient market explanation, then there is the puzzle of why many such patterns have continued to work out of sample (even though we will discuss one metric that stopped working once discovered).

4.2.1 Examples of Governance indicators

I will start our discussion with Governance—the last of ESG's three letters. Governance is often overshadowed by its flashier Environmental and Social companions and is all too often taken for granted. That's unfortunate, because the materiality of Governance to the underlying business is often clearer than that of either Environmental or Social characteristics. By "materiality" I mean the significance of a given piece of information to the risk or valuation of a given asset; or, if you prefer, the likelihood that investors would find this information relevant to their decision making. Governance is also more universal because it is likely material for all companies we may trade. In contrast, E and S may be material only for some specific sectors. For example, the Sustainable Accounting Standards Board (SASB) suggests that none of the environmental issues they consider are relevant for commercial banks.[10] And while there are probably some investors who look at banks' environmental profiles, most investors likely do not, and this information may not have a large influence on banks' valuation in the stock market.

Moreover, since Governance is generally agreed to be important, we have a longer history of research in this field than for other sustainability issues.

One example is a paper published in 2003 that used 24 indicators to define a "governance index" to proxy for the level of shareholder rights.[11] For every company that the researchers studied, they analyzed whether the company had provisions that restricted shareholder rights. For example, some companies may have supermajority merger rules, golden parachutes, or provisions that stagger elections of directors, and hence can be used to slow down strategic changes within a company. The researchers then sorted the underlying firms into portfolios, placing firms in the worst governance decile in the "Dictatorship Portfolio," and firms in the best governance decile in the "Democracy Portfolio."

Before I tell you what the results were, what do you predict? Would you expect higher returns on the Dictatorship, or on the Democracy firms? Think back to our discussion in Chapter 3 of how markets price ESG and specifically to Figure 3.1 in that chapter. Your answer should depend on whether you think we are in an ESG-unaware, ESG-aware, or maybe even ESG-motivated market. Since this research paper used data from the 1990s, before ESG became the talk of the town, it is perhaps plausible that this was still an ESG-unaware market. And indeed, over the period studied in the paper, the Democracy portfolio handily beat the Dictatorship one. You can see the difference in returns in Figure 4.1. Please note that the original study used data through 1999 only.

I have another question for you: what do you think happened next, once the study was published? If you peeked at Figure 4.1, you already know the answer, but allow me to go over the reasoning. The original study became known around 2000. Chances are at least some investors were convinced by its findings (perhaps because the study ticks many of the "good paper" guidelines I mentioned earlier in this chapter). Some investors may have even started to trade on this information, trying to capture the

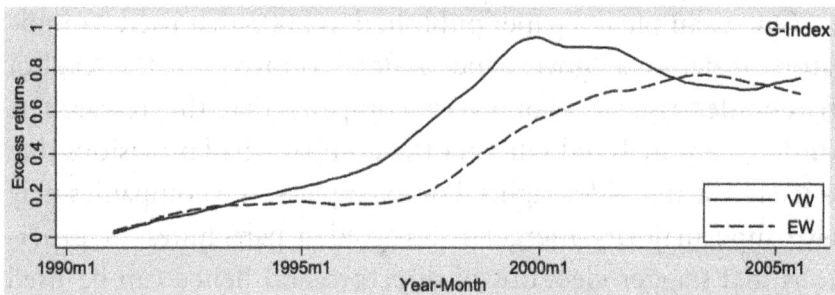

Figure 4.1   Markets learning about the value of governance. The "VW" and "EW" show the difference in returns between portfolios holding Democracy and Dictatorship companies. In the "VW" portfolio, companies are value-weighted (larger companies have a larger portfolio weight); in the "EW" portfolio, each company has equal weight.

Source: Bebchuk, L.A., Cohen, A., and Wang, C.C.Y. (2013). Learning and the disappearing association between governance and returns. *Journal of Financial Economics*, 108 (2): 323–348.

return premium the research had demonstrated. This means that the market plausibly started to move from ESG-unaware to ESG-aware.

A few years later, another group of researchers followed up on this study.[12] First, they replicated the original finding. I cannot emphasize how refreshing it is. Replication is critically important, but sadly, it is not as richly rewarded in the academic publication process as is documenting a new result. And indeed, this study's key contribution was something else: it showed that the effect disappears in the few years following the original sample. Figure 4.1 shows you the trajectory of the effect.

The study ascribes this to markets learning, which is basically the same statement I made about the transition from an ESG-unaware to an ESG-aware environment. The study even provided some additional evidence supporting this conjecture: around the time of the repricing, there was a coincident increase in media references to corporate governance.

While the governance indicator lost its power to predict returns, we should not conclude it became unimportant. The likely reason why it stopped "working" is that valuations started to reflect governance. That is, Democracy companies become relatively more expensive and, as we learned in Chapter 3, now have somewhat lower expected returns than they used to. In contrast, Dictatorship companies become cheaper and now have relatively higher expected returns. The market shifted so that you can no longer earn a return spread between the two companies, just as we saw in the "ESG-aware" line in Chapter 3, Figure 3.1.

Interestingly and surprisingly (to me at least), the market does not seem to learn quite as quickly about many other indicators. Here is another one, based on the idea that well-governed companies tend to be more conservative. To measure conservatism, we can look at the firm's financial statements and gauge the quality of its earnings.[13] One of the most famous ways to do so is to assess how much a firm relies on accruals. Formally, an accrual corresponds to revenue earned or cost incurred in one accounting period, but not realized until a future accounting period. For example, a firm may have provided a service and billed the customer, but has not received the payment yet or, conversely, may have purchased supplies but has not delivered payment to the supplier yet. There is nothing inherently wrong with accruals. In fact, they are critically important to painting the full picture of a company's business. Nonetheless, accruals are riskier than cash in hand (perhaps a customer that owes you payment defaults in the meantime) and they also give the management more leeway for creative accounting (it is more difficult to be creative with cash, other than outright fraud, I guess). So, let's take a look at the measure defined as overall accruals divided by total assets.[14] We will label firms that rely less on accruals as "well governed" and firms that rely more on accruals as "poorly governed," at least when it comes to conservatism, which as we discussed is one important facet of Governance.

So, how do better-governed firms fare, compared to their poorly governed peers? Panel A of Figure 4.2 answers the question by sorting firms into quintiles based on our governance metric and then computing their returns in excess of the overall market return.

Panel A suggests that investors focusing on strong governance can indeed earn excess returns: the 20% of the firms that rank best on our governance metric outperformed the overall market by about 1% per annum (in Panel A, we are looking at developed market large-cap stocks, and the market index is the MSCI World index). Conversely, the 20% of stocks with poor governance underperformed the benchmark index by about 2% per year.

A nice pattern in returns is a necessary first step, but as I've already hinted, a prudent investor would want to see more than just a single chart (or a single regression, etc.). How can we convince ourselves that there is indeed something here? One key test is looking out-of-sample: do the results still hold after the time period considered in the original study? The answer is yes, not just because of the many papers that have replicated the original evidence, but also because Figure 4.2 is itself an out-of-sample replication. The original study established this result using stock returns between 1962 and 1991, while Figure 4.2 reflects the 1990–2017 period.

But there's more. Another way to look at a different sample is to consider if the investment idea holds for different securities. We started with stocks, but we can also look at corporate bonds. Panel B of Figure 4.2 again sorts firms into quintiles based on our governance measure, but this time it shows the returns on the corporate bonds issued by those

Panel A: Application to public equities

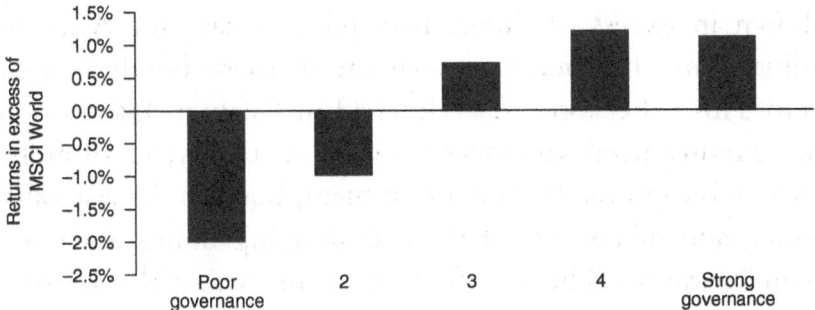

Panel B: Application to corporate bonds

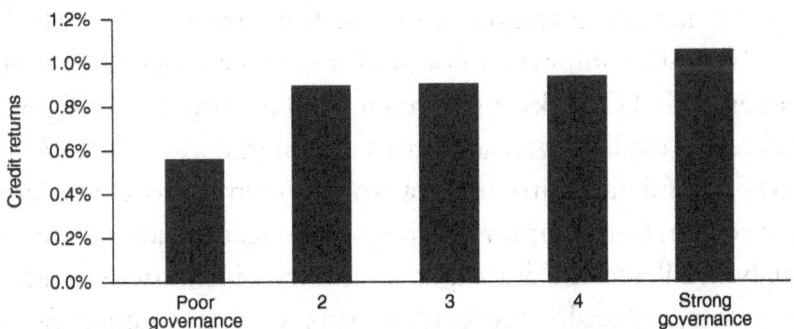

Panel C: Application to sovereign bonds

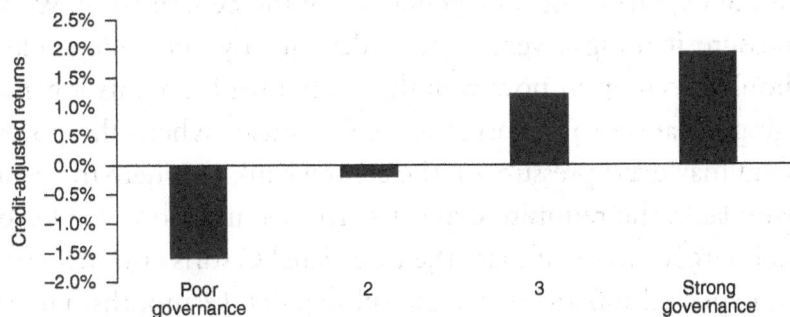

Figure 4.2 Predicting stock, corporate bond, and sovereign bond returns using governance indicators. Time periods depicted are 1990–2017 in Panel A, 1996–2019 in Panel B, and 2003–2018 in Panel C.

Source: Responsible asset selection: ESG in portfolio decisions. (2019). AQR whitepaper..

firms. To adjust for variation in interest rates, bond returns are shown in excess of duration-matched Treasuries. After this adjustment, the average return on all these bonds is above zero. This is because, as we learned in Chapter 3, the overall bond return needs to reflect not only the time value of money (which is captured by Treasury returns) but also the risk of the issuer, and of course, all these underlying bonds are riskier than Treasuries. The key finding, again, is that the return is higher for bonds issued by well-governed companies, relative to bonds of poorly governed issuers.

An additional insight we glean from Figure 4.2 is that the "G" in ESG is important not just for corporate, but also for other issuers. Panel C looks at sovereign fixed income to see if governance may explain average returns also in that asset class. We need to be careful here. First, our governance metric above was defined for corporations, not for sovereigns. We need to adjust it accordingly. We'll use the idea that a country's institutions matter to investors, especially the central bank of that country. So, one important component of governance at a country level should be the expertise and independence of the central bank. We will measure it using a very simple idea: quality and independence should show up in how well the central bank does its job, managing inflation to its target level. Countries where the government may exert pressure on the central bank or where the central bank lacks the requisite expertise may see inflation well beyond their targets. To see if that's the case, Panel C sorts countries based on expected inflation over the subsequent 12 months. The second nuance is that we analyze emerging markets here. To be sure, governance is very important for developed markets, but there is much less country-to-country variation in governance than we see between individual emerging countries. Finally, since there are many fewer countries than stocks, Panel C bins emerging countries into quartiles rather than quintiles. The overall result is similar to what we saw in Panels A and B: tilting a portfolio toward bonds issued by well-governed emerging countries has paid off in higher returns.

After this short sovereign detour, let's come back to corporate issuers. I want to stress once more that investors who develop their investment views should test their ideas as much as possible before they invest in them, incurring transaction costs and putting their capital, or their clients' capital at risk. So, let's test our accruals-based governance metric further. We have already seen that it predicts returns over different historical periods, and that it works for both stocks and corporate bonds. We will now try to understand *why* it works. That is, if the market is ESG-unaware, what exactly is it missing? What is the connection between the ESG idea we study and firms' fundamentals?

Let's think about it. We deal with governance here, and specifically with conservatism. What could happen to actors who are less-than-conservative? Since our measure is based on financial statements, the risk is that more aggressive accounting assumptions may force a firm to restate its earnings in the future. Indeed, there is evidence that this happens more frequently in accruals-heavy firms. A possibly even more serious scenario is that the SEC may initiate an enforcement action against the firm—and indeed, the data confirms that this, too, is more frequent for accruals-heavy companies.[15] Restatements and SEC enforcement actions are bad news for the stock price, contributing to the pattern we saw in Figure 4.2 (even though there are likely other, less egregious risk outcomes of poor governance).

We can zoom in even more by assessing individual case studies. At this point, we are going from systematic evidence to anecdotes, but these anecdotes can still enrich our understanding. So, we may want to go over individual companies that had particularly severe governance and financial statement mishaps and check if our measure would have helped to identify such companies before the event occurred. The standard here should not be the perfect hit rate—predicting controversies is difficult, and a signal may be very valuable even if it only picks up some such events. For our final illustration of governance, we will revisit what is arguably the biggest governance scandal in recent financial history: the bankruptcy of Enron, which not only was ruinous to the firm's shareholders but also took down one of the most storied auditing firms at that time, Arthur Andersen.

Figure 4.3 computes our governance metric (accruals over assets) for Enron in the few years preceding its bankruptcy.[16] In interpreting the chart please note that financials are released only with a lag: Enron's fiscal year end was 31 December, so investors would have learned about the 2000 financials early in 2001. We can see the increase in accruals—for the three years preceding bankruptcy, they exceeded 10% of the company's total asset. For comparison, in the years depicted in the figure, Enron's net income peaked in 1996 at 4% of total assets; in the firm's last three years, it ranged from 2% to 3.3% of total assets. If anything, you might ask why it took so long for Enron's share

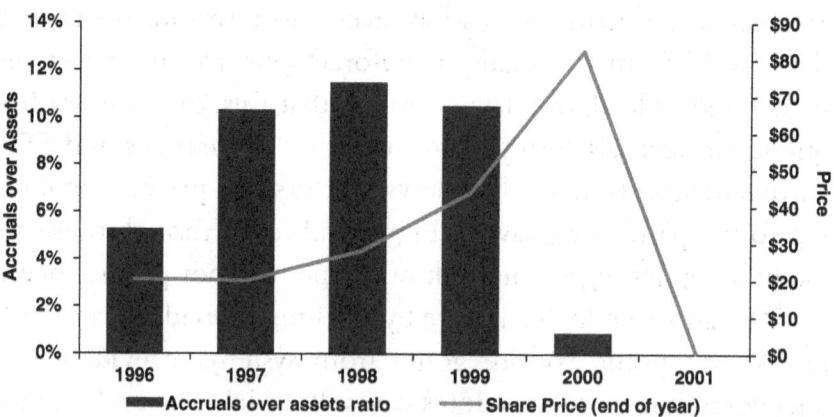

Figure 4.3   Enron's accruals and share price.

Source: Data from Richardson, S. (2003). Earnings quality and short sellers. *Accounting Horizons*, 17: 49.

price to plummet—and you'd be in good company if you did; for example, there is no evidence that short sellers were onto the firm's shenanigans until shortly before the firm went bankrupt.[17]

We went over our governance metric at length, covering test after test after test. I hope all this evidence was not too overwhelming, but I wanted to send a strong message. To build a plausible investment case for any metric, ESG or not, you may need to show a lot of sweat and go well beyond documenting that returns correlate with your favorite ESG measure. At least, you should. Generating risk-adjusted returns really is difficult, and if you think you can do that just because of a single returns regression, you are likely rolling a die with your money or, worse still, with your clients' money.

Before we move on to Social indicators, a comment on the governance metrics we discussed here. These metrics may seem somewhat obscure, and if you polled investors about governance, they probably would not be at the top of the list. That's kind of the point though. I wanted to showcase data that captures some facets of governance that are important for the firm and its shareholders. At the same time, I wanted to show you indicators that predict (or at least predicted) returns. This constrains my choices. For example, some of the most obvious Governance indicators do not seem to correlate with returns, possibly because they are well-known to the market and already incorporated into security prices.[18]

4.2.2 Examples of Social indicators

As an example of a Social indicator, we will consider employee satisfaction, which tells us how well the firm takes care of its employees. As with our discussion of Governance, let's start with materiality: could this metric matter for valuation, and could it affect the investment choices of a typical investor in the market?

I believe that the answer is "yes." Happy employees are likely to be more motivated to work and might even work harder for relatively lower wages than they would in less-employee-friendly firms. Companies with happy employees may also have an easier time recruiting requisite talent and face less personnel turnover.

This is all well, but how can we measure employee satisfaction? You might wait for a labor-related controversy (e.g., a lawsuit or a whistleblower), but these are relatively rare and only identify the laggards, rather than the firms that are doing particularly well. You could try to interview employees of a given firm, but this method is labor intensive and does not scale well (although if you're thinking about setting up a website to do this, you'll see in a page or two that you're on to something!).

We may need to be creative, as was an important paper that proposed that we leverage the Fortune 100 "Best Companies to Work For" list for this purpose.[19] This is a list that *Fortune* magazine has been publishing in cooperation with Great Place to Work for over a quarter century. The list is based on global surveys that are meant to capture "trust in management, connection with colleagues, and loyalty to the company."[20] The Social metric we can create is quite simply being on the list (a sign of attractive Social characteristics), or not being on the list (which indicates that the firm's Social characteristics are neutral or maybe even negative). The study then assessed whether companies on the "Best to Work For" list had higher average returns than companies not on the list. Amazingly, they did, beating their peers by 2–3% per year over the period 1984 to 2011. The study took this as evidence that the market did not fully recognize the value of intangibles, such as employee satisfaction. So, once more, we seem to see an example of an ESG-unaware market.

The study did not stop at establishing this pattern in returns, which is a good thing—as we have already seen, we need more evidence to build up our conviction and ideally give us a sense of *why* the data works. We started this section with a discussion of why employee satisfaction may be material for the firm. The possibilities that we outlined all imply higher profits, either because of employee's higher productivity or because of lower costs that the high-satisfaction company may deal with. If these conjectures are true, then we should see a pattern not just in stock returns, but also in earnings announcements that are surprisingly positive to the market. This is just what the study found. The "Best to Work For" companies experienced higher earnings surprises than peer firms over the two years following getting on the Forbes list.

The evidence from returns and earnings is convincing, but I have one more important piece of the puzzle. A few years after the study just discussed was published, there was another paper that further reinforced its results.[21] Here, as well, we see an ingenious data strategy: to understand employee satisfaction, this paper leveraged crowd-sourced employer reviews from Glassdoor, a website designed to gather and disseminate such information. However, while the first study looked at the level of satisfaction (a company either was or was not on the Forbes list), the second paper looked at changes in the employees' rating of their firm. This makes sense: we know from Chapter 3 that the market reacts to new information, so zeroing in on improvers and laggards may lead to a stronger effect. It's not to say that the original paper made a mistake. It did what it could with much coarser data (basically, an indicator variable, only available at the annual frequency). As you may expect, firms with increasing employee satisfaction do much better, in the near term at least, than firms with decreasing employee satisfaction. It seems that the channel here is indeed information flowing from employee reviews to the market, because this effect is concentrated among reviews from current employees and is stronger when the employee works in the firm's headquarters state. It is also stronger among early firm reviews, again suggesting that the market reacts most strongly to new information releases. As in the first study we discussed, there was a link between employee reviews and subsequent earnings surprises; reviews also predicted growth in sales and profitability. The study concluded that *"the evidence is consistent with employee reviews revealing fundamental information about the firm."*[22]

4.2.3 Examples of Environment indicators

4.2.3.1 Carbon emissions

We will start with the most prevalent of all environmental indicators, and arguably the second most important piece of data after ESG ratings: greenhouse gas emissions. Data providers convert the greenhouse potential of various gases to a common unit, expressing the overall emissions of an issuer in tons of CO_2-equivalent (carbon dioxide-equivalent). For example, over the course of a century, methane is roughly 30 times more potent as a greenhouse gas than CO_2, so one ton of methane counts as 30 tons of CO_2-equivalent. Because of this convention, greenhouse gas emissions are often informally referred to as "carbon emissions." This data is typically assessed for corporate issuers, but emissions are also estimated for sovereigns, municipalities, etc.

An important feature of corporate emissions data is that it is reported in scopes. Scopes capture where the emissions occur in relation to the firm. Loosely speaking, Scope 1 are emissions from assets controlled by the firm itself; Scope 2 are emissions behind the purchases of energy by the firm; and Scope 3 refer to the supply chain, capturing the emission traceable to the supplies the firm uses and to the firm's customers using its products and services. For example, if you consider Tesla, emissions from a factory that Tesla owns would qualify as Scope 1; if Tesla buys electricity from a utility firm, then the greenhouse gas emitted to generate that electricity counts as Scope 2; and emissions needed to generate electricity Tesla customers put into their cars go to Tesla's Scope 3. Of course, carbon accounting is much more complex than this simple example suggests, and there are thick manuals on estimating these quantities.[23] For example, the Technical Guidance for Calculating Scope 3 Emissions (Version 1.0) alone counts 182 pages, and this guidance is merely a supplement to the Corporate Value Chain (Scope 3) Accounting and Reporting Standard.

For the moment, we will focus on the sum of Scope 1 and Scope 2 emissions, which is the quantity that the vast majority of climate investors use. We will return to Scope 3 emissions at the end of this chapter. For now, suffice it to say that this category is much more difficult to estimate and is not nearly as popular in investment practice as Scope 1 and 2 emissions.

When it comes to Scopes 1 and 2, there are multiple ways to use this data and a few different formulas investors commonly use in practice.[24] In this book, we will focus on what's becoming a de facto standard in this space: carbon footprint. Carbon footprint apportions the greenhouse gas emissions of portfolio companies to their investors, prorating emissions based on each investor's fractional ownership, typically reflecting both equity and bonds. For example, if a company emits 50 million tons of CO_2 and an investor holds 5% of that company in their portfolio, then this investor's carbon footprint from that company is 5% of 50 or 2.5 million tons of CO_2.

Before we start working with the carbon footprint, we need to spend a bit more time on due diligence of the emissions data, just as I admonished investors to do earlier in this chapter. First, let's discuss where this data actually comes from. It turns out that much of the carbon data is reported directly by the emitting firms themselves. They may publish this data in their own disclosures, perhaps in Corporate Social Responsibility (CSR) reports, or report it to aggregators such as CDP (an organization we will take a closer look at in Chapter 5). As a rough estimate, nowadays, perhaps three-quarters of large firms in developed markets and maybe half of large firms in emerging markets report their own emissions. I stress "large," as in firms that belong to core stock market indexes such as the MSCI World or MSCI Emerging index. Smaller firms do not report emissions nearly as frequently—perhaps only 20% of them do.

Not surprisingly, self-reported emissions are deemed to be more precise than those estimated by a third party. So, in the vast majority of cases, providers of carbon data simply report the same values as the underlying firm reports. This may not seem like much, but the value of a provider is really in estimating emissions for the companies that do not report. Providers use a variety of methods to do so, including peer comparisons or more complex economic models.[25]

Now that we know more about the data, we should attempt to assess its quality. In a way, this is easier than for ESG ratings, because there is some objective truth we are after: how much greenhouse gasses a firm emitted in a given year. Still, we rarely observe that quantity directly. Instead, we may need to resort to indirect tests. For example, since we agree on what it is we are trying to measure, comparisons of data provided by different providers make more sense than for ESG ratings. It turns out that the carbon data is very consistent across providers. Let's start with the data for the companies that report their own estimates. As I mentioned earlier, these estimates are typically reported by providers as-is. Indeed, a study of five different data firms reported correlations of about 97% between providers.[26] This may not seem impressive, since the providers all have the same source. If anything, you may ask why the number is not 100% exactly. My own discussions with providers indicate that in a very small minority of cases, providers may override company-reported data that the provider deems to be suspicious.

More interestingly, we can look only at those companies that do not report their own estimates. For these companies, emissions from the five data providers are 72% correlated. The two leading providers in this space, MSCI and S&P Trucost, are 88% correlated. These numbers are not 100%, of course, but they indicate not just a positive relationship but also a stronger relationship than we saw for ESG ratings.

One more thing that our due diligence may unearth is that by the time carbon data gets to investors' hands, it is surprisingly stale. Think about it: to know what a firm's profit was, you usually need to wait a few weeks after the quarter end for the firm to announce its financials. Even in those jurisdictions where firms report only annually, you will typically know the annual profit weeks or, at most, months after the end of the fiscal year. But with carbon, you need to wait meaningfully longer. If you access corporate emissions data early in a year (say, at the end of the first quarter of 2024), the vast majority of firms will only have emissions data for 2022. Providers will typically update their data throughout the year, but even at the end of 2024, they may only have 2023 emissions for perhaps three-quarters of the firms they cover. There are multiple reasons why that is. For example, firms may report their own emissions in CSR reports published in the summer of the following year (e.g., the report that discloses their 2023 emissions may only be published in the summer of 2024). Many firms report to aggregators such as the already mentioned CDP, but CDP only releases their surveys for a given year in the fall of the next year. Finally, data providers themselves may want to wait for enough firms to publish their own estimates before the provider starts to estimate the emissions of the non-reporting firms. This delay is, on average, about 1.5 years, and there is a nontrivial minority of datapoints (perhaps

10%) that are delayed by 2 or more years. Moreover, when I say that the delay is 1.5 years on average, I mean that the data capture emissions in the year that ended 1.5 years ago, so the greenhouse gasses were actually emitted between 2.5 and 1.5 years earlier.

This means that when we build or invest in a low-carbon portfolio, this portfolio is informed by which companies were green or brown two years earlier, not necessarily today! Many investors are surprised by these figures: it is commonly known that the data is historical, but few investors carry out even the simple analysis we are going over here, and so few appreciate how long the delay actually is.

Luckily, there is a remedy: we could try to use all the data at our disposal and try to predict what emissions portfolio companies have today. Before we build a complex "nowcasting" model, let's start with the simplest possible approach: assuming that company emissions are constant over time. This is clearly not the case in practice, but we may as well try it out as a research exercise. We can frame this exercise in very practical investment terms:

Step One: build a low-carbon portfolio using carbon data that's available today (with the understanding it captures emissions firms had 1–2 years ago).

Step Two: learn what the emissions of the portfolio companies are today.

Step Three: compare the emissions you thought your portfolio companies had, based on the data you used in Step One, to the actual emissions you learned in Step Two.

Sounds simple, although you probably already picked up the obvious problem in Step Two. We've just seen that we do not know companies' emissions today—the best we can do is emissions a year or two ago. But we're doing research here, and research sometimes allows us to peek into the future. For example, put yourself in the shoes of an investor in December 2020, and start with the data that were actually available to investors at that time. Build a green portfolio from this data, for example, targeting a 50% reduction in the carbon footprint, relative to the carbon footprint of a broad market benchmark.

Now, the time machine part: look ahead to the data in the year 2023. No actual 2020 investor could do that, but you, the researcher, can. By 2023, companies will have reported their own 2020 carbon emissions or the data providers will have estimated those. Armed with this knowledge, you can come back to your 2020 portfolio and measure its carbon footprint using the actual 2020 emissions of your portfolio companies.

And if you do, you will probably be surprised. At least, I was when two coauthors and I ran that experiment.[27] It turns out that those stale historical emissions we get from data providers are amazingly close to the actual emissions portfolio companies had in the portfolio formation year. That is, the portfolio you came up with in 2020 is not only green using stale data (which few investors would find impressive), but more importantly, it is also green based on the actual 2020 emissions of your portfolio companies (which is ultimately what investors care about). Of course, emissions do change over time, and portfolios based on historical data may overshoot slightly in one year and undershoot in another. Also, emissions can clearly massively change for any one company. But, in a diversified portfolio of many companies, this company-level variation largely cancels out. Overall, our research found that the difference in the carbon footprint based on historical data, relative to the carbon footprint based on these look-ahead emissions, is only about 4% on average.

The good news here is that investors can then build portfolios using historical data, and still legitimately call these portfolios "green."

The bad news is that the reason for this surprisingly close alignment is quite sobering. Companies' historical emissions are close to emissions today because the economy as a whole is very slow to decarbonize. Stale emissions are still a good guide to today's emissions because firms do not change their behavior much over a couple of years. To put this in context, consider the COVID pandemic and the massive global intervention it led to. You might expect that no flying, working from home, etc. led to a meaningful change in global carbon emissions. In reality, their drop was not even in double digits: official estimates suggest that global emissions in 2020 fell by about 6–7% compared to the year before.[28] Remember this green portfolio we built in December 2020? If you actually built it in 2020, you may have been aware that the data you used captured emissions in 2018 or maybe 2019, and that they must have been higher than what your portfolio companies actually emitted in 2020. But, even in that extreme case, the difference between the two turned out to be quite small, perhaps depressingly so.

Of course, these findings may change if and when the pace of decarbonization picks up. But at least now we know what to look for, and we can rerun the above experiment over time to see how much the delay in reporting distorts the picture.

As the last part of our due diligence, let's look at the distribution of emissions across companies. Doing so will give us a better sense of the data but also, as we will see, will have important implications for portfolios that use this data.

Figure 4.4 works with a value-weighted portfolio of the largest 2,000 stocks in the world (value-weighted means that we allocate capital to stocks depending on their total market capitalization, so that larger stocks get higher weights in the portfolio). This portfolio is conceptually similar to a broad market index. We can then compute the carbon footprint of that portfolio. Figure 4.4 decomposes the total, portfolio-level carbon footprint into individual stocks, sorted by their contribution to the overall

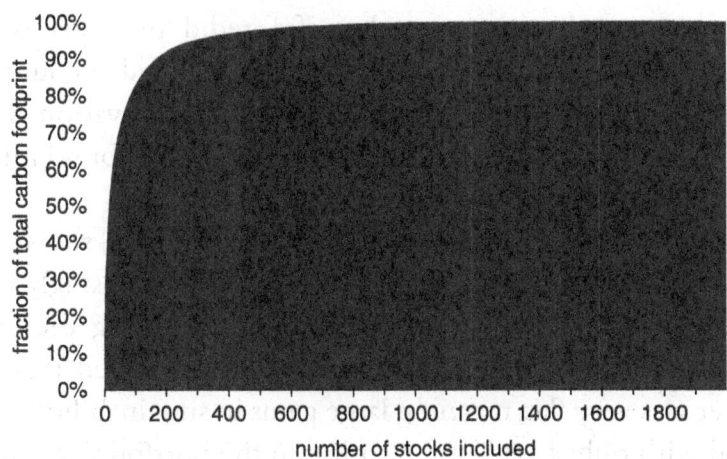

Figure 4.4 Distribution of individual stocks' carbon emissions. The chart shows the fraction of the total portfolio carbon footprint that is driven by a given number of stocks in the portfolio. The portfolio is value-weighted over the 2,000 largest stocks in the global equity markets (developed and emerging).

portfolio, from the brownest on the left to the greenest on the right. The chart shows how many stocks you need to account for 10% of the total portfolio footprint, how many you need for 20%, 50%, 90%.

Figure 4.4 has a very particular shape. The biggest emitters have disproportionately large contributions to the portfolio-level footprint. Shockingly, it turns out that you only need 20 stocks (1% of the total) to account for half of the portfolio's carbon footprint! The 200 stocks with the highest contribution (so, 10% of the total number of stocks) account for about 90% of the total portfolio carbon footprint. This is not an artifact of a carefully chosen example. You see the same extreme skewness in many other portfolios or indexes, even in stock markets that are relatively greener. Figure 4.4 reflects both developed and emerging stocks. The latter are, on average, much more carbon-intense—but if I redid this exercise in developed markets only, then 2% of stocks would account for over 50% of the total carbon footprint. This observation is not just an interesting bit of trivia but actually has profound implications for green portfolios.

Recall Figure 2.4 from Chapter 2. The figure shows the ESG efficient frontier for portfolios that seek increasingly high carbon reduction versus a benchmark index, using the same data we are analyzing here. In Chapter 2 we noted that the frontier was very flat, meaning large gains in sustainability could be had with only a small degradation in the portfolio's financial attractiveness. We are now in a position to explain why that is the case. The key driver is the skewness in emissions. If you can halve your carbon footprint by removing a small number of stocks from the portfolio, then you shouldn't expect a large change in portfolio attractiveness. Moreover, the way you build this portfolio effectively combines both the purely risk–return view of each stock, with the stock's carbon emissions. Suppose one of these carbon-heavy companies happens to be very attractive on purely financial grounds. You could then decide to retain it in the portfolio and deliver on your low carbon tilt by not holding the next two or three carbon-heavy stocks, at least, assuming that their expected returns are not as attractive.

4.2.3.2   Carbon penalty or carbon sin premium?

The last point we need to cover is whether firms' carbon emissions carry any information about expected returns. This question is hotly debated. Moreover, the markets may still be coming to terms with how to price emissions. For this reason, we will not be able to conclusively address the question. What we can do, though, is use the frameworks we have developed so far in our book and at least outline and explain three potential investment views one may have:

1. Green firms may outperform brown ones: there is a repricing of climate risks and opportunities, but it is still incomplete.
2. Green firms may underperform brown ones: there is excessive climate repricing, or climate repricing is complete and there is a carbon risk premium.
3. Green firms may deliver similar risk-adjusted returns as brown firms: climate repricing is complete but it is not excessive, and/or there is no carbon risk premium.

The first view (green firms are positioned to outperform brown firms) is fairly popular in the financial sector. There are many proponents of this view, but perhaps the most famous one is Blackrock's Larry Fink, who in his 2020 letter said that *"Our investment conviction is that sustainability- and climate-integrated portfolios can provide better risk-adjusted returns to investors."*[29] We can map this statement to the ESG-unaware market scenario we considered in Chapter 3. There are two necessary ingredients to this view. The first one is that emissions correlate with firm fundamentals, perhaps because brown firms face climate risks that may lead to lower expected profits (e.g., maybe they will need to pay a high carbon tax). The second ingredient is that this information is only slowly percolating in the market and that the prices today may not fully reflect it. Advocates of this view may bring up the fact that some green indexes have outperformed broad market indexes. For example, as of the end of 2023, MSCI World Paris-Aligned Index has outperformed its broad-market equivalent, MSCI World Index, by about 0.8% per year over the preceding decade. If repricing is indeed incomplete, then one could expect such relatively higher returns also going forward.

The second view (green firms will do worse, on average, than brown firms) is more popular in academia. This view corresponds to the ESG-motivated market we considered in Chapter 3. According to its proponents, climate repricing is now complete.[30] The market has adjusted prices not just to reflect the potential for the low-carbon transition, but pushed them even further to reflect the changing investor tastes. During this repricing, green firms did well (their prices increased relative to the prices of brown firms). According to this view, this is exactly why we have observed high past returns on green indexes. However, going forward, we should expect a sin premium and relatively higher returns on brown securities. I should note that a variant of this view is that there is a systematic climate risk premium that you can earn by holding brown securities, which presumably have more climate risk exposure.

Finally, the third view is middle-of-the-road. Markets have repriced climate exposures, but not so excessively that there is now a carbon sin premium (or perhaps a carbon risk premium). According to this view, the expected returns on green or brown securities will be roughly similar going forward. In any given year, one or the other may randomly outperform, but positioning your portfolio toward green or toward brown stocks should not be expected to change your long-term performance.

I admit the third view appeals to me the most. It seems unlikely that markets keep underreacting to information about climate and decarbonization, given how heavily discussed these topics have been in recent years. I do allow that some aspects of climate may be underappreciated (more on this later), but I expect the markets have already priced in at least the most obvious exposures. At the same time, I'm not yet ready to declare that there is a sin premium. Again, markets may not be fully efficient, but there are still a lot of investors who are willing to buy fossil fuels if the price is low enough. We already saw in the last chapter that sin premia may not be quite as obvious as one might think, even when investors had multiple decades of shunning some industries. We will see another example in the next chapter when we compare the pricing of green and ordinary bonds—there is a difference between them, but it amounts to just a few basis points per year (a basis point is one-hundredth of one percent).

But, ultimately, these investment views are just that—views. We will validate them over time, but in the short term, I don't expect smoking gun evidence that will conclusively demonstrate that one of them dominates.

4.2.3.3 Using weather data to predict agricultural commodity prices

Of course, corporate greenhouse gas emissions are not the only "E" data that investors may be interested in. As another example, we could try using information about weather patterns to predict asset returns. The classical application is to use such data to explain and forecast commodity prices, with a financial application to commodity futures trading. (More on these contracts in Chapter 6 and, for readers interested in old comedies with a financial angle, in the 1983 hit movie *Trading Places*.) But there are applications also in trading equities. The idea is that if weather patterns help you predict the prices of agricultural goods, we may also be able to forecast the prices of food, beverage, and agricultural companies. This is exactly what one research paper did.[31]

To forecast returns on food stocks, the paper used a weather indicator called the Palmer Drought Severity Index (PDSI). PDSI uses temperature and precipitation data to estimate relative dryness in a given geographic region. The investment idea is then to sell food stocks in countries with negative PDSI trends, which forecast low agricultural yields. At the same time, you would buy food companies in the countries where PDSI predicts bountiful harvests. This strategy does well over the 31 countries considered in this study, suggesting markets underreact to weather- and perhaps also climate-type information. As before, we would want to have more than just returns evidence. Luckily, the study had additional robustness analyses. Importantly for our intuition, it also investigated the mechanism, documenting that PDSI trends help explain the food industry profitability.

4.3   Building our own ESG data

We'll finish this chapter with a case study that will help us see how many of the challenges discussed earlier can be met, and how a new ESG metric can be built and tested.[32] As we argued before, investors interested in ESG may be best served by identifying specific aspects of ESG that they care about, and then looking for dedicated data to measure those aspects. For example, an investor may be interested in climate and have the broad goal of managing a portfolio's climate exposure. We already know that such an investor has a wide array of data at their disposal. Earlier in this chapter, we discussed broad ESG ratings that include "E" as one of their components and typically have climate-related themes within "E." We also talked about carbon emissions data, and it is not much of a stretch that stocks with high carbon emissions may be relatively more exposed to climate risk. These metrics could be a great starting point, but may not fully capture all of a firm's climate risk. Notably, the data we mentioned here may not reflect any potential climate exposures along the firm's supply chain.

Such supply chain climate exposures may matter. For example, think about a technology company specializing in payment services. The company's industry, IT Services, is not typically associated with climate risk. Moreover, if we look up the usual ESG and climate data for the firm, it may look relatively attractive. Perhaps its carbon emissions are low even compared to the company's industry peers (who are already much greener than companies in many other industries). All this looks promising until we look at the company's customers—perhaps in the firm's 10-K reports, which by regulation must disclose major customers of a public firm. Suppose the 10-K indicates that the firm's top three strategic relationships are with major oil companies and that these companies account for 20% of the firm's overall revenue. This could change our assessment. Climate change risk might manifest as (say) a global carbon tax. This might be immaterial for a typical IT services company but may be crippling for oil majors. But if some IT firms rely on oil majors for a significant portion of their revenue, then they too may be exposed indirectly. They may experience disruption and potential loss of revenue when climate risks manifest for their clients.

At this point, the investor might conclude that their investment process would benefit from data describing stocks' supply chain climate exposure. How can we deliver on this need? The most straightforward way would be to obtain such data from a reputable ESG data provider. You may remember from our earlier discussion that company carbon emissions come in scopes. We already discussed Scopes 1 and 2, but maybe we can now leverage Scope 3 emissions, or emissions traceable to the supplies the firm uses or to how the firm's customers use its products and services. This explicit supply chain focus seems to be a good match for what we are looking for.

By now, we know the drill. Before we put capital at risk using this data, we should carry out some due diligence. First, I said earlier that investors generally prefer emission estimates reported by the portfolio company itself. Unfortunately, relatively few companies report Scope 3 emissions, and those that do typically only report some selective categories. For example, the Greenhouse Gas Protocol subdivides Scope 3 emissions into 15 different categories. Of these, many companies only report category 6 (business travel) and maybe also category 7 (employee commuting), and do not report any of the categories related to the supply chain. Moreover, some companies are vocal that Scope 3 emissions are very difficult for them to estimate. For example, IBM's 2020 Environment Report stated that *"the assumptions that must be made to estimate Scope 3 emissions in most categories do not enable credible, factual numbers."* Since companies may not report this measure, you could try to use estimates from data providers. Unfortunately, it seems that providers' Scope 3 estimates are also very noisy and they differ meaningfully provider to provider, with a correlation of only 16%.[33] Recall that for the broad ESG ratings, the correlation was 54%, and even that was too low for some commentators.

Given this information, you may be averse to using Scope 3 data in your portfolio. You would not be alone. In the 2020 ESG survey published by Callan, a consultant, about 12% of respondents said they had explored carbon footprint portfolio measurement. Of these, about 60% implemented Scope 1, and about 40% implemented Scope 2. However, 0% of respondents implemented Scope 3. I do hope that eventually, we may improve carbon accounting to the point that Scope 3 estimates become more precise. But today this is not yet the case, at least not for the broad cross-section of firms an investor may want to trade.[34]

But if you decide against using Scope 3 data, you are not left with many choices—most ESG data providers have no other climate measures that focus on the supply chain. You can either give up on the idea or try to develop your own measure. And if you choose the latter, you will need to not only propose a measure, but ideally also validate it (due diligence, once more!).

My co-authors and I were precisely in this situation a few years ago. We came up with the idea that a firm's supply chain climate exposure depends on how much business that firm does with carbon-heavy companies. This can be measured as a revenue-weighted average of customers' standalone climate exposure, and a cost-weighted average of suppliers' standalone climate exposure. I hope you see this as an intuitive idea. For example, our measure will indicate high supply chain exposure for a firm when some of the firm's customers have very high climate exposure, and/or when the firm does a lot of business with climate-exposed customers.

Let's think back to our example of a payment services firm (which is actually based on a real-world company). That firm derived 20% of its revenues from oil majors; let's assume that the remaining 80% came from average companies. To compute the supply chain exposure of the payment services firm, we would then take 20% of oil majors' standalone exposure (which presumably is a high number) and 80% of the typical company exposure. To measure the standalone exposure of each customer, you could use your favorite climate metric—in our study, we used the Scope 1+2 carbon emissions of each customer.

Now, onto due diligence. The measure was designed to capture climate risks, so our tests should reflect it. This turns out to be a formidable challenge. We rarely observe climate risks directly, at least for the time being. They may be quite serious in the future (indeed, that's why we worry about climate risk), but our historical data does not include enough major climate events on which we could test our measure. Instead, we needed to establish a plausible link between our measure and potential future risks that have not yet materialized. Our first step in that direction was essentially a smell test. We checked that our data has intuitive patterns across sectors and geographies. For example, our measure spikes in fossil fuel industries. This makes sense because, almost by definition, customers of fossil fuel companies consume fossil fuels and the more important a customer, the more fossil fuels they purchase and presumably process within their business. We also looked at the correlation between our measure and a variety of third-party climate metrics. As we discussed, the one standard metric that should capture the supply chain, Scope 3 emissions, is very imprecisely estimated, but there may be other data that might at least partially reflect the supply chain. For example, many ESG ratings providers also publish climate preparedness scores that feed into their ratings. We documented that our measure had a positive but small correlation with such metrics. This was a welcome finding. If we had found very high correlations, our measure would not be interesting on its own—you could simply rely on those third-party metrics. Also, if we found no correlation at all, this would be bad news about our measure. Climate data providers are experts in their field, and while their metrics may be noisy, they likely capture at least some relevant information. If you introduce a new measure that is unrelated to any existing metrics, then either you found something completely novel (possible, but in my view unlikely), or your own metric may be extremely noisy, to put it mildly.

Our most convincing validation came from a simple idea. Climate risks may only materialize in the future, but after all markets also look into the future, based on all information that may be relevant for the assets they trade. This must include information about climate. So, if we can identify new climate information as it arrives in the market, we could then test our supply chain measure against it. To do so, we used a climate news sentiment proposed by an earlier study. The sentiment data looks at newswires and identifies which articles talk about climate through a machine learning technique called topic modeling. Once you identify the relevant documents, you can then measure the sentiment of their language to hone in on positive climate news (e.g., breakthroughs in green technology) or negative news (e.g., a country delaying previously planned fossil fuel regulations). If such news is important enough, then you should expect markets to price it accordingly. In this example, green firms should do relatively better when positive climate news is released, and brown firms should beat their green peers when there is negative climate news. The key question is whether green and brown companies, identified using our measure, show such a pattern in returns. It turns out that they do. Moreover, we verified that this pattern is not explained by other, third-party climate data. We concluded that our measure contains information that is relevant when the market reacts to climate news, and that this information is not subsumed by other sources of data.

The final test that we ran used a hand-collected sample of major events that had a climate component. For example, the 2016 US presidential election is one such event. Donald Trump's win came as a surprise to the market and, given the then-candidate's vocal view on climate, had likely shifted the expectations about green and brown stocks' trajectory. Indeed, during this and other similar "event studies" we saw intuitive repricing patterns in the green and brown stocks, as identified by the measure we proposed. This additional evidence that our measure helps explain (co)movement in green and brown stocks further reinforced our conviction that it, in fact, captures climate-related information.

Note that when discussing the tests, I have not mentioned expected returns. Our goal was to identify a measure of risk exposure, not necessarily a potential alpha factor. Of course, once we had done all that work, we also looked at returns. We found some tantalizing evidence that the exposures we identified may not be fully reflected in market prices and that there may be a potential to incrementally forecast returns using our measure. But, I stress again, this is not why we built it—although it is certainly nice that the project yielded some additional side benefits.

Notes

1. Friede, G., Busch, T., and Bassen, A. (2015). ESG and financial performance: aggregated evidence from more than 2000 empirical studies. *Journal of Sustainable Finance and Investment*, 5 (4): 210–233.
2. For a more in-depth discussion of third-party ESG ratings, see Larcker, D.F., Pomorski, L., Tayan, B., and Watts, E.M. (2022). ESG ratings: a compass without direction. Stanford Closer Look Series.
3. Alves, R., Krueger, P., and van Dijk, M.A. (2023). Drawing up the bill: is ESG related to stock returns around the world? Working Paper, University of Geneva.
4. Dimson, E., Marsh, P., and Staunton, M. (2020). Divergent ESG ratings. *Journal of Portfolio Management*, 47 (1): 75–87. For a more in-depth discussion of how to attribute performance of ESG-focused indexes and funds, see, for example, Horan, S.M., Dimson E., Emery, C., Blay, K., Yelton, G., and Agarwal, A. (2022). *ESG Investment Outcomes, Performance Evaluation, and Attribution*. CFA Research Foundation.
5. For example, you can look up individual company MSCI ESG scores at https://www.msci.com/our-solutions/esg-investing/esg-ratings-climate-search-tool, or Sustainalytics ESG scores at https://www.sustainalytics.com/esg-ratings
6. Dunn, J., Fitzgibbons, S., and Pomorski, L. (2018). Assessing risk through environmental, social, and governance exposures. *Journal of Investment Management*, 16 (1): 4–17.
7. MSCI (2024). Equity factor models: redefining the way models are constructed and delivered. https://www.msci.com/our-solutions/factor-investing/factor-models
8. Berg, F., Koelbel, J.F., and Rigobon, R. (2022). Aggregate confusion: the divergence of ESG ratings. *Review of Finance*, 26 (6): 1315–1344.

9. See, for example, Diether, K.B., Malloy, C.J., and Scherbina, A. (2002). Differences of opinion and the cross section of stock returns. *Journal of Finance*, 57 (5): 2113–2141.
10. See https://sasb.org and their industry materiality topics, for example at https://sasb.org/standards/materiality-finder/find/?industry%5B0%5D=FN-C
11. Gompers, P.A., Ishii, J.L., and Metrick, A. (2003). Corporate governance and equity prices. *Quarterly Journal of Economics*, 118 (1): 107–155. If you are interested in the underlying data, it is available on Professor Andrew Metrick's website, https://faculty.som.yale.edu/andrewmetrick/data/
12. Bebchuk, L.A., Cohen, A., and Wang, C.C.Y. (2013). Learning and the disappearing association between governance and returns. *Journal of Financial Economics*, 108 (2): 323–348.
13. Hopefully this idea makes intuitive sense, but if you want to analyze this in more detail, one relevant reference could be Kim, Y., Park, M.S., and Wier, B. (2012). Is earnings quality associated with corporate social responsibility? *The Accounting Review*, 87 (3): 761–796.
14. This measure was proposed and validated in Sloan, R.G. (1996). Do prices fully reflect information in accruals and cash flows about future earnings? *The Accounting Review*, 71 (3): 289–315 and several subsequent papers. You may wonder why we normalize accruals by assets rather than earnings. The answer is that the accounting value of assets is positive, which earnings can be negative at times, which would make the ratio more difficult to work with.
15. The evidence on accruals can be found in Richardson, S., Tuna, A.I., and Wu, M. (2002). Predicting earnings management: the case of earnings restatements. Working paper, University of Pennsylvania, and on SEC enforcement actions in Richardson, S.A., Sloan, R.G., Soliman, M.T., and Tuna, A.I. (2006). The implications of accounting

distortions and growth for accruals and profitability, *The Accounting Review*, 81 (3), 713–743.

16. The data comes from Richardson, S. (2003). Earnings quality and short sellers. *Accounting Horizons*, 17: 49.

17. Ibid.

18. I am guessing that if we polled investors about Governance indicators, many would suggest board diversity, and the number of women on boards. This would make my point. There are many reasons to support board diversity, but higher expected returns are not one of them. The interested reader may read the excellent testimony on the topic that Professor Alex Edmans gave to the UK's Financial Reporting Council: https://alexedmans.com/wp-content/uploads/2019/02/Diversity.pdf

19. Edmans, A. (2011). Does the stock market fully value intangibles? Employee satisfaction and equity prices. *Journal of Financial Economics*, 101(3): 621–640.

20. See https://fortune.com/franchise-list-page/best-companies-2023-methodology/

21. Green, T.C., Huang, R., Wen, Q., and Zhou, D. (2019). Crowdsourced employer reviews and stock returns. *Journal of Financial Economics*, 134 (1), 236–251.

22. Ibid.

23. Interested reader may want to consult the greenhouse gas protocol, https://ghgprotocol.org/corporate-standard

24. A good reference is the former Taskforce for Climate-Related Financial Disclosures, or TCFD. Their website includes a number of helpful documents, explaining the typical metrics investors are encouraged to use: https://www.fsb-tcfd.org/. See also the IFRS website, https://www.ifrs.org/sustainability/tcfd/, which continues the TCFD's mission.

25. For more information about carbon data, and for deeper analyses than those we summarize in this chapter, see, for example, Bixby, S., Brixton, A., and Pomorski, L. (2022). Looking forward with historical carbon data, In E. Jurczenko (ed.), *Climate Investing: New Strategies and Implementation Challenges*, pp. 29–48. Wiley and ISTE.

26. Busch, T., Johnson, M., and Pioch, T. (2020). Corporate Carbon performance data: quo vadis? *Journal of Industrial Ecology*, 26 (1): 350–363.

27. Bixby, Brixton, and Pomorski (2022), cited n. xxv.

28. IEA. (2021). Global energy review: CO_2 emissions in 2020. https://www.iea.org/articles/global-energy-review-co2-emissions-in-2020

29. See https://www.blackrock.com/corporate/investor-relations/2020-larry-fink-ceo-letter

30. See, for example, Bolton, P. and Kacperczyk, M. (2021). Do investors care about carbon risk? *Journal of Financial Economics*, 142 (2): 517–549, or Pastor, L., Stambaugh, R., and Taylor, L.A. (2022). Dissecting green returns. *Journal of Financial Economics*, 146 (2): 403–424.

31. Hong, H., Li, F.W., and Xu, J. (2019). Climate risks and market efficiency. *Journal of Econometrics*, 208 (1): 265–281.

32. This section is based on Hall, G., Liu, K., Pomorski, L., and Serban, L. (2023). Supply chain climate exposure. *Financial Analysts Journal*, 79 (1): 58–76.

33. Busch et al. (2020), cited n. xxvi.

34. Estimating Scope 3 may be easier for specific industries. For example, we have good estimates for emissions released from a barrel of oil, meaning we can likely estimate at least that part of oil companies' Scope 3 emissions.

Chapter 5

Can ESG Investing Change the World?

S o far, we have discussed how investors incorporate sustainability into building their portfolios: how they decide which securities to buy or to sell, pursuing their purely financial but also potentially nonfinancial objectives and preferences. In this chapter, we discuss what investors do *after* they've built the portfolio: how they interact with the issuers of the securities they hold and under what circumstances they may influence the issuers' real-economy activities. We will decode the jargon investors typically use in this context ("proxy voting," "engagement," "impact") and try to parse the often cryptic and, unfortunately, muddled claims one hears in this space.

Engagement and impact predominantly refer to corporate issuers (and to investors who hold stocks and corporate bonds), so we begin with a refresher on corporate governance. We will review how corporations are run, the important delineation between ownership (equity holders) and control (corporate officers), and the tools the former have to communicate with and ultimately influence the latter. We will then discuss how these tools are used in practice and review the evidence showing that they indeed have impact—that is, that they can lead to measurable changes in corporate activities and in stock valuation. We will also introduce the increasingly popular type of security: green bonds (or labeled bonds more broadly), and we will see how these instruments can lead to achieving the impact investors desire.

To further put these concepts into practice, we will discuss the increasingly popular push toward "net zero": using financial ownership to influence issuers to reduce their greenhouse gas emissions, contributing to economy-wide climate objectives.

One topic we will leave for our next chapter is impact in non-corporate asset classes. This is one of the more hotly debated issues in this nascent field. After some decades of discussions and hands-on experience, investors are increasingly comfortable with impact via corporate stocks and bonds. However, they now increasingly think about their overall allocations, including sovereign bonds, illiquid asset classes such as private equity or infrastructure, hedge funds, or instruments such as commodity derivatives. Their sustainability goals are being redefined across these asset classes, often leading to conceptual problems and heated debates. One such timely issue is whether short selling "counts": could it be used by sustainability-oriented investors, could it plausibly have impact, or even how to report on sustainability characteristics of a portfolio that includes short positions? The next chapter will shed light on these issues, hopefully making them less confusing—although it is probably realistic to expect that they will still evoke strong emotions.

But, for now, let's start with building a foundation by focusing on traditional portfolios that hold stocks and (corporate) bonds.

5.1   Corporate Governance Refresher

When we talk about "a corporation," we often implicitly mean a whole ecosystem of actors, operating within a set of rules referred to as corporate governance. As we will see shortly, the quality of governance is an important driver of firm value and a focus of many investors. This absolutely holds for ESG investors—indeed, the "G" in ESG urges investors to consider the quality of governance in their investments.

A key concept in our discussion will be the separation of ownership and control. The owners of the corporation are the equity holders (or shareholders). However, they do not oversee the day-to-day operations of the firm. That task is delegated to the corporate management team: the Chief Executive Officer (CEO) and the senior managers who work with the CEO. Since this separation may lead to frictions between the owners and the agents, the latter are overseen by the board of directors. The board is tasked with ensuring that the management works to maximize shareholder value: the value of the equity they hold, usually measured by the share price.

Besides the shareholders and corporate management, the corporate governance ecosystem includes various stakeholders who interact with the company. They may include the firm's creditors (banks that make loans to the firm, or bondholders, who hold bonds issued by the company), but also employees, suppliers, customers, or advisors who support the board and the overall corporation (for example, the auditors).

On the one hand, the separation of ownership and control is desirable. Most importantly, it allows the firms to seek financing from a diverse group of investors, raising more capital, on more attractive terms, than they could have otherwise. Raising capital from a narrow group of investors is usually more difficult. First, few investors may have enough capital to satisfy the firm's financing needs. Second, even if they do, their resulting portfolios may be under-diversified: they may be disproportionately exposed to a single firm, exposing their portfolios to risk if the firm does poorly. Even if the investors are willing to tolerate such risks, they will likely expect a return premium—in other words, they will demand a higher cost of capital that the firm would need to pay.

On the other hand, the separation has a major drawback. The interests of principals and agents are rarely perfectly aligned. Unfortunately for shareholders, they have neither the information nor the resources to monitor the management's every action, every day. The agents (corporate officers) may then decide to exert less effort than the principals would prefer, or may prioritize projects that give the management benefits that do not accrue to shareholders. We refer to such tensions as agency issues.

There are many examples of such behavior. An oft-cited example is building an empire, or engaging in highly visible projects that give the management team more stature even if they do not add much value to the shareholder. A CEO may be attracted to a glamorous acquisition, literally increasing the size of the empire he or she commands, even if the synergies the acquisition promises are, at best, elusive. Indeed, academic research has found that the average acquirer experiences a drop in valuation,[1] suggesting that, on average, investors view planned acquisitions skeptically. Readers who seek more examples may consult *Barbarians at the Gate*[2] for an account of particularly egregious agency conflicts.

5.1.1 Stakeholder capitalism?

Let's assume for the moment that investors and corporate managers are perfectly aligned and that there are no agency issues of the sort described earlier. It turns out that even in this (rather unrealistic) corporate idyll, there will be potential frictions between the two parties. It all comes down to the question of what specific objective managers should be responsible for.

This question is more challenging than it may appear and some seemingly intuitive answers turn out to be deeply flawed. For example, maximizing profits may not be appealing because it may lead to low investment and potentially lower future profits (indeed, many CEOs have been accused of short-termism and of inflating the bottom line for just one reporting quarter or year!). Lowering costs is even worse: you may lower them to zero by dissolving the corporation and returning the capital to shareholders. Clearly, that's not what most shareholders would want.

Of course, many readers may immediately point out that the objective should be to maximize the shareholder value (think about the price of each share, multiplied by the number of shares outstanding). There are multiple benefits to this approach. First, it is very relevant for shareholders since it directly measures the value of their stake in the company. Second, this measure is arguably more objective than many alternatives, in that it represents the collective wisdom of the overall market. As we saw in Chapter 3, the market is very adept at seeking and aggregating information into prices. Third, it is readily observed by the management and by all market participants, and thus can serve as a timely barometer of corporate decisions, even those that may only lead to profits many years down the road. Because of these advantages, shareholder value is enshrined in our corporate system. Corporate officers are explicitly expected to take actions they believe maximize shareholder value, and boards of directors oversee the management with the same goal in mind.

Of course, no measure is perfect and one can identify situations in which maximizing shareholder value does not lead to best economic outcomes, especially when corporate decisions lead to externalities. Externalities are side consequences of economic decisions that affect other stakeholders and that typically are not captured by the prices of goods and services a company produces.

For an example of why maximizing shareholder value may not be ideal, consider a firm with a production process that generates toxic waste.[3] For the purposes of our example, let's assume that the firm can either legally deposit the waste in a nearby lake, or build a costly treatment plant that would process the waste into harmless chemicals. If the management of the firm wants to maximize shareholder value, they will prefer the former to the latter. The reason is simply costs: dumping waste into a lake is cheaper than investing in the treatment plant. With lower costs, the firm's profits will be higher and hence the overall firm value will be higher as well (again, please note we are assuming the firm can legally dump the waste and that it won't be exposed to potential fines, consumer boycott, etc.). The standard argument, going back to the classic Milton Friedman's article on the primacy of shareholder value,[4] is that this behavior is perfectly fine. The firm maximizes how much it is worth to investors. Investors are richer than they would have been otherwise, and if they want to invest part of their wealth in other objectives, that's perfectly fine. In this example, shareholders who care about the environment might donate to an environmental charity to make up for their investment in the polluting firm.

This may seem a reasonable idea until we realize that the increase in corporate profits (i.e., the cost savings of not building the treatment plant) may be much smaller than the cost of cleaning up the lake after the waste is already deposited there. If the owners of the company care about a clean environment, then they may well be better off if the company invests in the costly treatment plant. Yes, the value of their investment would then be relatively lower, but they would not need to spend as much money on environmental cleanup. The shareholder-value-maximizing alternative may well leave them poorer overall.

This is a powerful example. It illustrates that when there are externalities, then maximizing shareholder value could distort overall economic outcomes away from what asset owners would rationally prefer. Of course, there is nothing special about the environmental context into which we put our example. It is easy, perhaps depressingly so, to come up with similar examples for a variety of other issues. Think about a social media company that maximizes user engagement and does not pay attention to the psychological damage it might cause some subset of its users. This course of action could be the best way to maximize shareholder value, but may clash with other shareholder needs. Perhaps some shareholders decide to forbid their children from using the company's product in its current form. They may have been happier overall with a lower shareholder value and with a product that generates less profit but serves their community better. As you may have noticed, this argument works even though we only considered the wellbeing and preferences of shareholders. You could extend this reasoning to also include other stakeholders, for example the firm's employees, customers, etc.

Given how pervasive such issues are, it's not surprising that there is ongoing discussion about moving away from shareholder value and explicitly incorporating other stakeholders' interests in corporations' goals and objectives (hence, "stakeholder capitalism"). Perhaps the most vivid example of this movement was the 2019 Business Roundtable Statement on the Purpose of a Corporation. The Statement was signed by 200 CEOs of the largest corporations in the United States, and the gist of the agreement was that firms should account not just for shareholders' interests but also for those of customers, employees, suppliers, and the broader communities in which the firms operate.

While the statement reflected the prevailing sentiment at the time, it drew immediate criticism. Within a day, *Pensions & Investments*, a trade journal, published an editorial with a telling title "Well-intentioned, maybe, but wrong." Indeed, some flaws in the statement are fairly apparent. For example, it is by no means clear how to measure the collective interest of all the various stakeholders that a company directly or indirectly interacts with. We faced this challenge in Chapter 4, where we discussed how difficult it is to build a summary measure that would capture all ESG-related dimensions an investor might care about. Even if it is possible to come up with informative measures of how a firm influences its stakeholders, such measures are almost surely going to be subjective. Some well-meaning analysts or data providers may put more emphasis on employees, others on the environment, and so on. As with ESG ratings, this is not necessarily a bad thing since different people may well care about different issues. However, the inevitable disagreement about the measures could lead to a diffusion of responsibility. It may be possible to defend just about any corporate decision by appealing to *some* such measure, or perhaps explicitly to some specific stakeholder interest, even if the decision harms other stakeholders—and shareholders in particular. Moreover, while we are better at recognizing the weaknesses of shareholder value, it is not clear how stakeholder capitalism solves these issues. For example, think back to the firm that dumps toxic waste into a lake. Of course, we want to avoid such situations, but it may well be easier to do so by thoughtful regulation that directly addresses the externalities a firm creates, than by redefining the purpose of the corporation.

Overall, it is unlikely we will move away from shareholder value any time soon. At present at least, it is difficult to think of a realistic alternative that would be nearly as simple, timely, and—dare I say—objective. Moreover, there is also an even more powerful, if prosaic, reason for the dominance of shareholder value: its pivotal role in the current regulation. It is what guides the work of corporate officers and the boards that oversee them. As long as the current regulation binds these key actors to maximize shareholder value, they can hardly manage to other metrics. To be clear, this does not mean that sustainability has no place in the corner office or in the boardroom. Quite the contrary, corporate officers and boards should absolutely think about other stakeholders to the extent there is an impact on shareholder value. Emitting toxic sludge into a lake could lead to reputational damage or, if regulation changes, fines to the firm. Social media companies that do not think about the externalities of their products may eventually face consumer backlash and diminished revenue. And so on. Many investors believe, perhaps correctly, that in some cases corporations are simply unaware of, or do not fully appreciate, the link between the two. That may well be the case, but if so, then the complaint should be that the management team does not maximize the value for its shareholders, and not that it should take on the goal of addressing a different stakeholder's interests.[5]

5.2   Proxy Voting

Broadly speaking, the separation between ownership and control limits shareholders' involvement with their companies to two channels: voting and engagement. The former is more widespread and typically open to all shareholders of record, whether they are individuals or institutions. Voting usually takes place at the annual shareholder meeting, typically over a range of standard topics that include director elections, advisory votes on compensation, etc. This may also include votes on shareholder resolutions or proposals brought by individual shareholders for the firm to consider—we will see some examples shortly. Less frequently, firms reach out to their shareholders to vote on major corporate decisions, for example, mergers and acquisitions.

How do investors know how to vote on each item on the ballot (or indeed whether to vote at all)? This is a formidable challenge. An institutional investor may easily hold thousands of voteable securities in their equity allocation. An investor who passively replicates an index such as MSCI World may hold some 1,500 stocks; if the investor also invests in the MSCI Emerging index, they might have another 1,400 or so stocks. Each of these securities may have multiple items on the ballot. Consequently, investors have the right to vote on a staggering number of issues every year. For example, Aviva, a major UK institution with a strong sustainability track record, reported that in 2022 it participated in about 6,500 shareholder meetings and voted close to 70,000 ballots.[6] Needless to say, this involves dealing with countries around the globe, frequently with different languages, cultures, and regulatory regimes. And Aviva is not a unique example. Many other asset owners and portfolio managers have similarly large voting programs.

Realistically, it would simply be uneconomical for most investors to spend the time and resources to build an informed view on how to vote every last share they own. If they wanted to do that, the required costs of the requisite talent, data, etc. would increase their investment costs to unsustainable levels (or, should they choose to pass these costs to their end clients, would make them uncompetitive). At the same time, many investors abhor the idea of sitting idly on their voteable stock.

This tension gives rise to proxy voting advisors, or firms that deliver recommendations on how investors may want to vote their shares. To play this role and deliver a comprehensive service, these firms need to develop a view on a vast range of corporate issuers, surpassing what even a large single institution may hold in its portfolio. To recoup the substantial cost of preparing such recommendations, proxy advisors need to attract enough clients willing to pay for the service. Perhaps not surprisingly, the resulting market is quite concentrated, with two institutions, ISS and Glass Lewis, accounting for the majority of the business.

Importantly for us, proxy advisors customize their services to investors with a range of ESG- and sustainability-related views. For example, along a standard policy that is meant to address most investors' needs, they may offer policies that reflect broad ESG preferences or adhere to religious values (e.g., both ISS and Glass Lewis offer Catholic faith-based voting guidelines) or policies focusing on specific issues such as climate change.

Delegating the decision of how to vote to a proxy services advisor may be economical to an asset manager but may also expose the manager to the criticism that they merely rubber stamp someone else's research. For this reason, some institutions may carry out internal research on at least some of its holdings, often focusing on those where the institution holds a larger fraction of voteable shares, where the item on the ballot is deemed relatively more important (e.g., a proxy fight, or a vote on a potential merger), or even where there is more divergence in views (e.g., when ISS and Glass Lewis offer conflicting recommendations).

Whether an investor relies on internal research or follows the guidance of a proxy advisor, an important question is whether voting shares, especially on ballots that matter for sustainability, makes any difference for the value of the investment. Research on sustainability-related shareholder proposals suggests that it does.[7] Teasing out the relationship is not quite as easy as simply looking at all proposals and recording the market reaction when a proposal passes or is rejected. This is because, in many cases, the result of the vote is hardly a surprise for the market. As it happens, most shareholder proposals are rejected, often by vote margins substantial enough to suggest that they were perhaps very unlikely to win to begin with. In such cases, market participants could have plausibly expected the outcome. When we discussed market efficiency in Chapter 3, we saw that markets price in all information as soon as it becomes available. So, if the markets expected that the vote would fail, we could see any potential impact on the price before the vote even takes place. Similarly, in those (fewer) situations when proposals pass by very large vote margins, market participants plausibly expected that and impounded this expectation into the price well ahead of the vote. This creates a challenge for the researcher. Not seeing a price reaction immediately after the vote might mean that votes have no impact, but it may also suggest that markets were able to correctly anticipate the result of the vote.

To resolve this difficulty, we can look at those votes that were too close for the market to plausibly call. When such votes are decided by a very thin margin on the day of the vote, this result was likely difficult to predict and comes as a surprise to the market. So, if such votes matter, then we should see a price reaction precisely at that time. And, it turns out, we do.

Figure 5.1 shows the change in stock valuations on the day of the vote. The horizontal axis is the vote margin: 0% is the exact tie (the same number of votes for and against a proposal), 50% means that the proposal passed without any votes against, -50% means that all shareholders voted against the proposal. As mentioned above, many ballots are decided by substantial

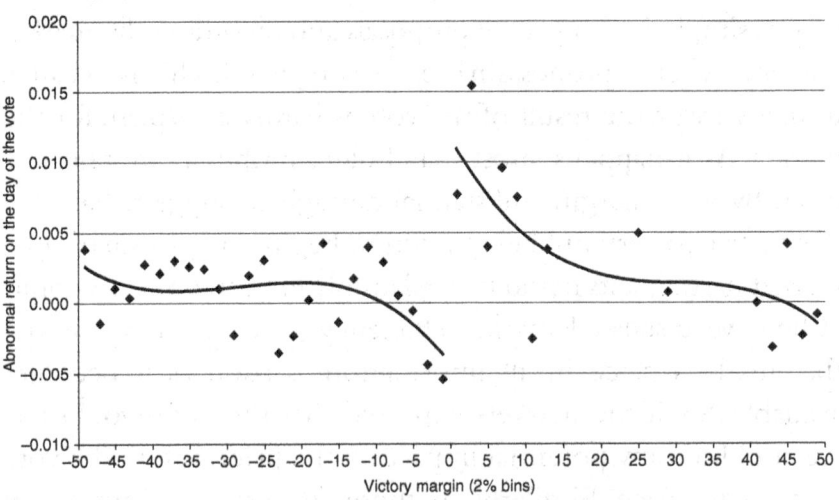

Figure 5.1 Changes in stock valuation following votes on shareholder proposal.

Source: Flammer, C. (2015). Does CSR lead to superior financial performance? A regression discontinuity approach. *Management Science*, 61 (11): 2549–2568. (c) IMFORMS.

margins of votes. Figure 5.1 suggests that in such cases, the change in firm value is indeed negligible: the dots, corresponding to individual votes, are scattered around zero.

More interestingly, the votes that were likely too close to call are associated with a stronger price reaction. The votes that barely passed (where the vote margin was positive, but very small) are accompanied by positive returns. Conversely, we see negative returns for the votes that barely lost (small negative vote margin). This suggests that the market prices sustainability, consistent with the evidence we already saw in Chapters 3 and 4. Here, we add to that evidence by showing that markets also react to investors' voicing their opinions about sustainability through votes on shareholder resolutions. The change in the valuation might seem small in Figure 5.1, but I would argue it is actually surprisingly material. We might see a 1% increase following a vote that just barely passes, or a 0.5% drop in valuations following a vote that barely loses. A typical company in a major stock market index has over $10 billion in market capitalization, so these numbers imply a change in company valuation of $50–100 million. Moreover, the change is driven not by a company actually adopting a sustainability-related policy, or even promising to do so. This is because shareholder resolutions are non-binding; they are merely forceful statements of shareholder concerns about a given matter. The fact that the markets react to them as strongly as they do suggest that companies indeed listen to their shareholders' voice and that when shareholders agree on a sustainability proposal, it is likely to increase firm value.

5.3 Engagement

Engagement is a more involved interaction between the investor and the portfolio company. Instead of voting a proxy, the investor requests a conversation directly with the firm, typically voicing a concern. The firm may concede, asking their investor relations team or, if appropriate, an executive to connect with the investor.

As with voting, investors who want to engage need to prepare ahead of time. They need to identify issues on which to engage and prepare an engagement plan that should have a specific measurable objective. Ideally, the investor also thinks about an escalation protocol in case some engagements turn out unsuccessful. All of this takes resources.

Luckily, not all firms are appropriate engagement targets. While voting occurs at least annually for most firms, issues that necessitate engagement may not be nearly as frequent. In addition, even if investors have concerns about a portfolio company, they may decide against engaging if the likelihood of success is relatively low—for example, if the investor only holds a very small stake in that firm.

All this means that the scope for engagement efforts is usually much smaller than that for voting. In a typical year, an institutional investor may vote in several thousand shareholder meetings, casting several tens of thousands of ballots. The same investor may only carry out a few hundred engagements per year. Even the largest institutions, with sizeable teams dedicated to engagement, may have engagements in the low thousands. For example, Blackrock's 2022 Stewardship report discloses that the investment firm engaged roughly 3,900 times, with 2,600 individual companies (some companies had multiple engagements).[8] This requires substantial scale: BlackRock's Investment Stewardship team has "70+ dedicated professionals, who work across 10 global offices." Many other investors scale down their efforts proportionally to how much resources they can devote to engagement. This is perhaps good news, as these fewer engagement opportunities may be better prepared and have a higher likelihood of success. Higher numbers are not always better: Even a small institution could artificially manufacture thousands of engagements by sending a mass email to multiple corporations at the same time. Such "engagements" would likely be only superficial and would have little chance of having the impact the investors, or the investors' clients, may want to have.

Those investors who do not have the necessary resources can collaborate on engagement with other investors. They might support another institution that takes a lead in the engagement, increasing the overall stake in the company that the investors jointly represent. Or, they may choose to use a pooled engagement service provider, who coordinates multiple investors' engagements for a fee.

Another popular model is to align one's engagement effort with a broader project led by a not-for-profit institution, such as CDP (formerly known as the Carbon Disclosure Project) or Climate Action 100+. Such organizations focus on specific issues investors care about (in the examples cited, climate) and make it easier for investors to identify appropriate targets for engagement and issues to engage on.

Let's consider an example. A popular goal of engagement is to increase the transparency of portfolio companies and convince them to improve their reporting on a given issue. This is particularly true for climate, as many investors are increasingly concerned with their portfolios' greenhouse gas emissions. Some investors then aim to identify companies with poor climate disclosure and appeal to these companies to provide at least partial reporting to the investment community. This channel of engagement is facilitated by organizations such as the above-mentioned CDP. CDP has an annual Non-Disclosure Campaign that attracts many institutional investors—for example, the CDP website lists close to

300 asset owners and investment managers who participated in the 2022 edition of the campaign. CDP sends these investors a list of non-disclosers, complete with the contact details. A light-touch investor may just sign their name to the campaign or perhaps use the CDP list to send a series of letters to the companies. Investors who want more hands-on engagements can reach out to the portfolio companies directly and explain why they believe climate reporting would benefit them and potentially also the broader investment community. Such engagements have a direct metric of success: we can observe whether the portfolio company starts its disclosure or not. For investors who work with institutions such as CDP, the not-for-profit may even help with tabulating engagement results.

Now that we know how investors may engage with portfolio companies, we need to ask whether engagement could possibly affect firm value. The answer is yes, just as with proxy voting, and here the evidence is even more direct. There is a class of investors, called "activists," whose investment process focuses precisely on engagement and attempting to change the underlying company. The typical activist investor identifies a target company and builds a stake that allows the investor to open a dialog with the company. The dialog may start friendly but could also turn hostile and result in a proxy contest. This happens when the activist demands one or more seats on the board of directors and proposes a different candidate than the company would prefer. If the activist wins the contest, the newly elected directors will presumably steer the company to address the weaknesses identified by the activist.

Not all activist campaigns may be clear to the public. The firm may decide to address the activist's concerns early on, without much fuss or media scrutiny. This may happen because the firm sees value in the activist's advice, or possibly because it wants to avoid the potentially negative media coverage or diffuse the risk of a subsequent proxy fight. However, many campaigns become publicly known through two key events. First, the activist may need to acquire a substantial stake in the firm to be able to change its course. When the stake exceeds 5% of all shares, regulation forces the activist to state so publicly through a Schedule 13D filing. Moreover, if the campaign leads to a proxy fight, these are again publicly observable—voting shareholders can clearly see the contesting directors on the ballot.

This means that the first time the market learns about an activist campaign is often when a new 13D is filed. The market reaction to such events is overwhelmingly positive: the stock price typically goes up by perhaps 5% on average.[9] This is a material change in the value of the firm. To understand this magnitude, we need to appreciate that activists do not approach random firms but rather identify those companies that they believe are particularly poorly run and where an intervention may be most helpful. Apparently, the market agrees—at least on the announcement date.

As you might expect, some people, perhaps including the management of target companies, may quibble with this evidence or prefer to interpret it differently. Activist investors are often accused of promoting short-termism, running pump-and-dump schemes, etc. To evaluate these concerns, let's start with our discussion of market efficiency. Markets should incorporate all new information, such as a 13D filing, and impound it into prices, to the extent it matters for the value of the company. If the new information is that an investor acquired a large stake only to liquidate it after the price increases, then it is difficult to see why the market should react to this positively.

Similarly, if the activist forces the company to pursue short-term projects at the expense of long-term growth, then, again, we should try to reconcile it with the price reaction we observe. It may be possible to do so. Even if the activist favors short-term projects, then perhaps the market considers them more attractive than the long-term projects the company had initially planned. In such a case, I could see why the activist intervention is expected to increase company value, but I would hesitate to call such behavior "short-termism."

But, it is also possible (even if unlikely) that the market could be repeatedly fooled when activists step in, increase the price of the target stock, only to see the price plummet after a while. To test if this is the case, researchers have looked at the long-term effects of activism in both stock price data and in the fundamentals of the underlying companies.[10] The data shows no indication of "pump and dump" kind of behavior. Quite the contrary: stocks with an activist intervention show subsequent improvements in their fundamentals, for example, they improve their return on assets (ROA) relative to their industry peers. To be clear, prior to the activist campaign, a typical target company had a meaningfully lower ROA than its industry peers. Again, activists focus on firms that they deem to be poorly run and that they believe can be improved. The good news here is that these firms, on average, go back to roughly industry-standard ROA within about three subsequent years. They may not become blue chip stocks, but at least they improve.

The point that activists select which stocks to engage with is an important one. It is highly unlikely that engaging with a random company would increase that company's value or its fundamentals. Activists target companies that trade at a discount, and the market reaction to a new campaign suggests investors believe that activists could indeed improve the underlying firm. This interpretation is supported by the kind of issues activist investors typically engage on. In most cases, the reason for the campaign is the general undervaluation of the target firm, and the course of actions activists seek usually has to do with changes in the capital structure, business strategy, sale of the target company, or general governance changes.[11]

The evidence we reviewed so far suggests that *some* engagements can affect company valuations. Moreover, the research on activists maps directly to engagements focusing on Governance, or the "G" pillar of ESG. What about the other two pillars, "E" and "S"? Historically, such engagements were relatively rare. Nowadays, as interest in sustainable investing grows, we see them more often, such that we now may have enough history of such engagements that we can start inferring some patterns from the data.

For example, a recent study analyzed close to 2,000 engagements by a single institution.[12] The engagements were roughly equally split into Governance-themed on one side and either Environmental- or Social-themed on the other. The former were similar to the activist engagements we analyzed earlier, with a focus on board structure, shareholder rights, transparency, etc. The latter were typical for how investors think about E- and S-pillars of ESG, dealing with climate change or ecosystem services for E, and with public health, human rights, or labor standards for S.

The most important part of the study was analyzing how engagements affect shareholder value. The authors followed target companies over the 18 months following the engagement, noting how well they performed. The key finding is that the price of a typical target appreciated by about 2% relative to how otherwise similar companies performed. Moreover, the authors looked separately at engagements that were successfully concluded and those that were not (as you may remember, a well-designed engagement should have a measurable goal). It turns out that the positive performance only accrued to the successful engagements, which appreciated by as much as 7% relative to peers. As Figure 5.2 shows, there is no indication that these price gains revert, at least not over the 1.5 years following the engagement. Unsuccessful engagements, on the other hand, did not experience any noticeable difference in performance relative to otherwise similar non-engagement stocks.

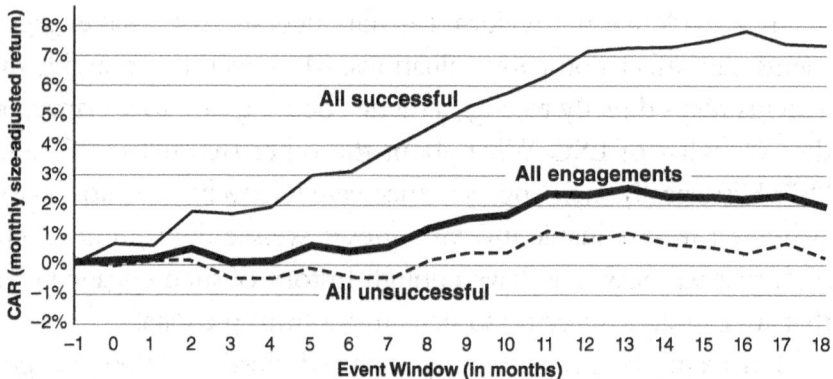

Figure 5.2 Performance of target companies in the 18 months following the engagement.

Source: Dimson, E., Karakas, O., and Li, X. (2015). Active ownership. *Review of Financial Studies*, 28 (12): 3225–3268.

These results suggest that engagement, including that focused on Environmental and Social themes, can positively influence company value. Moreover, the magnitude of the impact is again surprisingly large. Recall that a typical public firm may have $10 billion in market capitalization. If engagement indeed improves firm value by 7%, then a fruitful conversation between investors and corporate executives may add $700 million to shareholder value. That's a massive benefit, both to the shareholders who participated in the engagement and to the remaining ones, who may be wholly unaware of the interaction and are just enjoying the positive returns. This last point is important and often overlooked. You probably heard the adage that alpha (trading profits) is a zero-sum game: if an investor does well, then necessarily some other investor does poorly; when one person beats the market, there must be another person that underperforms by the same amount. That is true most of the time, and certainly when we talk about predicting future returns using ESG or other data, as we did in Chapter 4. However, engagement opens up a different and exciting possibility. If interacting with the company leads to an increase in firm value, then this benefits all investors who hold that stock, not just the one who actually engaged. This is a positive-sum game, because the engagement grows the pie for everybody involved.[13]

Now, before we take these results and urge all investors to engage more and more with their portfolio companies, let's think about this some more. Critically, we need to understand why some engagements are successful in the first place—recall that only such engagements are followed by discerningly positive returns.

First, perhaps the most obvious explanation is that the investor had a phenomenal idea that the company had been unaware of. Upon hearing the idea, corporate executives see its merit and implement it. That's possible, but perhaps overly optimistic. Investors, even those who are very savvy, typically know much less about the business of a specific portfolio company than does the company itself. One obvious reason is information: the firm has much more information about its suppliers, clients, and employees than an outside stakeholder would. Moreover, we have already mentioned that a typical institution holds thousands of investments, so its employees won't be able to spend as much time thinking about any single portfolio company as that company's executives would. So, I would not reject the "great idea" scenario out of hand, but I doubt it is very frequent. Moreover, I am very skeptical that this outcome can be easily scaled across the many firms in an investor's portfolio. It's unlikely a typical investor could keep coming up with brilliant business ideas that had been previously unknown to corporate insiders, and that insiders would then be happy to undertake. Obviously, if you find such an idea, you absolutely should act on it and engage with the relevant portfolio company. You will be increasing the value of your own investment and doing a favor to all other shareholders of that company at the same time.

Another possibility is that an engagement is successful because the company was already working on something related. Again, suppose that the investor has a good business idea and engages with the company on it. But this time the idea is not a surprise to corporate insiders. They have already thought about it, seen its potential value, and maybe even started incorporating it in their business practice. In such a case, the engagement will probably be a pleasure for both parties—they are on the same page from the get-go. Moreover, the investor will likely declare the engagement a success, because the firm is receptive to the idea. And if the idea indeed has merit, the market will eventually see it and drive up the stock price, increasing company value. In the end, all involved parties will be happy with the outcome. But, in this case, it is difficult to ascribe much value added (and certainly the entire value added) to the shareholders leading the engagement. The company had already been aware and perhaps working on the idea and it's not clear at all that the engagement itself changed any meaningful corporate outcomes.

The nuance we are highlighting here is the bane of much empirical research in corporate finance: we do not have a good way to assess the counterfactual, or what would have happened with the company in question without the engagement. It is possible that the key driver of the change in firm value is independent of the engagement itself, and engagement simply coincides with it. In other words, what we observe is correlation, but not causation.

As it happens, there are other ways to tell a similar story. For example, perhaps the company simply wants to acquiesce and is willing to agree with the shareholder even if they don't see any merit in the proposal. However, only those companies that are doing very well in their overall business can afford to do that. In this "ESG is a luxury good" scenario the companies that engage with investors may be those that are doing relatively better than their peers. When the market subsequently learns about their good prospects, it correctly increases the share price. Other companies cannot afford to spend resources on ESG and decline to act on the engagement. Here, a company's good fortune is the driver of engagement success, not the other way around. These "correlation, not causation" and "reverse causality" explanations are very difficult to empirically establish or to rule out, but I suspect that they account for at least part of the performance effect we saw earlier. Perhaps not the full effect, but I would not take the full estimate (such as the 7% we saw above) to measure how much value a successful engagement may bring.

Finally, and perhaps most interestingly, there is the case where shareholders and the company do not see eye to eye. Again, suppose that shareholders have what they deem to be a good idea for the company and talk to corporate insiders about it. But this time, the company does not see the value in the idea. This may be because (as we argued before) the company knows much more about its business and can assess the economic potential better than the investor. But it might also be that the investor is right, and the company is digging in its heels for motives other than shareholder interest. For example, an investor may be concerned that the CEO is too entrenched and that the board allows the CEO to behave in ways that benefit the corporate team rather than the shareholders. The corporate team might then push back against the engagement for fear of losing their rents, even if they understand the damage to shareholder value that they cause. (Clearly, what we are describing here is an example of poor governance.)

In this situation, could you still have a successful engagement? In other words, how can shareholders persuade the company to change its mind? This is an important question and, unfortunately, much of the popular commentary around it is muddled or even just plainly wrong.

5.4   Why Do Companies Listen to Their Investors?

Companies are clearly interested in talking to investors. Otherwise, the engagements we discuss here would be rare and not the fairly common occurrence they are in today's markets. Could the power investors have over companies persuade them not just to listen, but maybe even to agree to actions the company would otherwise prefer to avoid? To address this question, we will go over the economic incentives that come into play when companies interact with investors. In this context, there are only two channels of influence: first, direct control, for example through voting rights, and second, financing costs, or the price at which investors agree to provide capital to the company. There is nothing else that makes investors "special," and that gives them a seat at the table, as Figure 5.3 summarizes.[14]

As Figure 5.3 makes clear, control and financing costs are not the only ways to seek impact. For example, one could also try

1. Control	2. Financing Costs	3. Not Portfolio-Related
• Voting • Board representation • Direct control (e.g., PE)	• All portfolio decisions that influence the price of issuer's securities • Influencing issuance (e.g., labeled vs. regular bonds)	• Social outreach • Advocacy with stakeholders • Dialogue with regulators • ...
Function of portfolio holdings		No direct link to holdings

Figure 5.3   Different ways in which investors have influence on portfolio companies.

Source: Jones, B., Mendelson, M.A., and Pomorski, L. (2023). How portfolios can impact the real economy. AQR paper.

to influence the firm through direct outreach to its customers, perhaps persuading them to take their business elsewhere until the firm changes its ways. That is fine, but importantly one does not need a financial portfolio to do that. To the extent that investors seek impact that is somehow tied to their portfolios, or to their portfolio decisions, they explicitly or implicitly rely on either control or financing costs. And in what is one of many ironies in this space, they often talk more about the former but then build portfolios more aligned with the latter.

Of the two channels, control is more intuitive and decidedly more often discussed among the investment community. The underlying idea is very simple. If an investor owns the company outright, they have the full right to run it as they see fit (naturally, as long as they observe all relevant laws and regulations). Shareholders are owners, so even though they delegate the day-to-day management of the firm to others, it is natural that they exercise some measure of control through the votes they cast at shareholder meetings. For example, dissatisfied investors may decide to vote in board members who agree with their point of view, and these board members may then reshuffle the management team accordingly. Investors who want even more control may decide to seek direct board representation for themselves (as we saw in earlier pages with activist investors) or maybe even take the company private to be able to manage it more directly (as may happen with private equity). The control channel is particularly relevant with illiquid investments (private equity, real estate, infrastructure) where the investor, or a general partner who represents the investor, can more directly influence the day-to-day management of the underlying assets.

But the other channel, costs of financing, is also fundamentally important. Shareholders provide capital to corporations, mostly importantly during an initial public offering (IPO, when a company is listed on an exchange), but also at seasoned equity offerings (SEOs). They charge a price for this service in that they expect to earn a return on their investment; as we saw in Chapter 3, this expected return is a key determinant of the price of a given company. And when you take the perspective of the company, investors' expected return is nothing more than the company's cost of capital. To appreciate this, consider a stylized example of a firm that is trying to raise capital by issuing more shares in an SEO. For each share the company issues, an investor will pay the prevailing share price, expecting to earn some return in the future. If expected returns increase, this means that the share price drops and the company will raise less money per each new share they issue. Not surprisingly, companies are interested in keeping their cost of capital low, giving them an economic incentive to work with investors and potentially take actions to better align with investor needs.

For another example, consider corporate bonds. Corporate bonds are IOUs that companies issue to their creditors, promising to repay the capital they borrowed, with some interest. That interest is the cost of capital the company gets from bondholders. Companies are often eager to talk to their bondholders or to potential future bondholders, and maybe even address their concerns. Why do they do so? The answer is hopefully clear: in the hope that this reduces the interest rate the firm needs to pay. If companies are not willing to engage, then bondholders may sell their existing bonds (eventually depressing the bond prices and hence increasing the bond yields) and refuse to participate in future bond auctions. Importantly, there is no concept of "control" in this situation. Bondholders, dissatisfied or not, do not get a vote or board representation. So, they cannot influence company decision making in any way other than through the cost of financing. (In limited circumstances, bondholders may get some control rights, for example, when a company defaults on its obligations. But it seems a stretch to argue that bondholders have control over the company, or that companies want to engage with bondholders, specifically because of what may happen if and when the company goes bankrupt.)

Investors clearly influence companies' cost of capital, but we may not appreciate that they do so not just in the primary but also in the secondary market. In principle, all decisions to trade an asset may influence the price of the asset and may reflect changes to the expected return—and hence also to the cost of capital for that firm. This will be relevant whenever that firm chooses to raise new financing. The firm may do so through more issuance in that market, as in the stylized example above. But this may also influence the choice of the venue. The company may prefer to issue new equity, if only because historically, it paid a relatively lower cost of capital in that market. But if the cost of equity capital grows too high, then the company may now decide to instead seek financing through an issuance of bonds or through bank credit. And, of course, similar forces may also affect those other markets, and perhaps the investor will eventually need to pay more for financing even there.

While both control and cost of capital are important for the underlying companies, I should stress that these are two distinct channels and that they may manifest through different investor actions. For example, investors who want to maximize their control should concentrate their holdings in the equity of the firms they want to influence. This will give them more votes and potentially a way to get board representation, and is the strategy of choice for activist investors we described earlier. This is relevant both for investors who want to support the company and for investors who want to change its course.

In contrast, investors who want to maximize their impact through the cost of capital channel, may or may not behave in this manner. They may choose to stimulate the companies they are aligned with by providing them with cheap capital. This may involve acquiring a larger stake in the equity, but also potentially in other securities the companies issue—for example, as we have just discussed, in corporate bonds. Investors who disagree with the direction of a firm and want to increase the cost of capital, will go in the opposite direction. They will sell off their securities and not participate in any new offerings, in the hope that the prices drop and that the company raises less financing (or at least more expensive financing) in the future. There is a clear parallel between this mechanism and our discussion of sin premia in Chapter 3. The extra return investors may earn by holding stock of "sin" companies is nothing else than the additional financing cost such companies need to pay.

5.5   Case Studies

Let's apply these concepts to three practical illustrations of impact through investment portfolios. As an example of the control channel, we will discuss the proxy victory by Engine No. 1 and other investors that led to an unprecedented change in the composition of Exxon's board of directors. As an example of impact through the financing channel, we will consider green bonds, and finally we will study the investor movement to gradually reach "net zero" in investment portfolios.

5.5.1   Engine No. 1 and Exxon Mobil

When we covered voting and shareholder resolutions earlier in this chapter, I mentioned that they had rarely been successful. In fact, other than activist hedge funds, there do not seem to be many historical examples of investors driving major changes in their portfolio companies. Moreover, as we saw, activist hedge funds have not really been interested in sustainability per se (or, if they were, it was only the "G" in ESG). Arguably, this made some companies complacent: they did not believe sustainable investors could meaningfully influence major corporate events such as, for example, director elections.

This changed in the fall of 2021. A small and (until then) relatively unknown activist hedge fund, Engine No. 1, started a proxy fight with Exxon Mobil, one of the largest oil firms in the world. Engine No. 1 maintained that climate change and the likely transition to a low-carbon economy was a major threat to Exxon's business and that Exxon was not making enough efforts to address it. In fact, the activist maintained that the incumbent board of directors did not have sufficient expertise and experience to oversee the oil major's strategy in this important area. Consequently, Engine No. 1 formally nominated four candidates to Exxon's board who, the activist posited, would "bring a range of diversified energy experience required to protect and enhance the long-term value for shareholders." Investors voted and three of the four candidates were elected to the board.

How did Engine No. 1 achieve this feat? Importantly, it was not alone. It coordinated a major outreach to other investors, eventually building a coalition that counted 135 investors, jointly managing more than $2 trillion in assets.[15] Moreover, in its outreach and its director nominations, Engine No. 1 stressed long-term shareholder value. It described the changes proposed and the director nominees as essential to positioning Exxon's business in the dynamically changing world and argued that without such changes, the company is at a strategic disadvantage. This argument was persuasive enough to convince many institutions that voting alongside Engine No. 1 was aligned with the institutions' fiduciary duty—that is, that they were casting a vote to protect and maybe even grow their investment, not to achieve a climate goal that might otherwise be detrimental to their portfolio value. Moreover, it is important to stress that the newly elected directors are required to be guided by shareholders' interests and influence the firm's strategy to maximize shareholder value, whether it coincides or clashes with one's personal climate objectives.

So what happens now, and how much could the new directors change Exxon's direction? The short answer is that we do not know. First, it may be difficult to identify specific corporate decisions that are board-driven. Even if we could identify such a decision, it is possible it would have happened anyway, even without any changes to the board. In any case, some climate investors are disappointed by the actions Exxon has taken since then. They point to the expansion in Exxon's oil and gas production since then, or to the fact that green technology is still a tiny portion of the company's business. The president and chief counsel of As You Sow, an investor advocacy group, opined that the campaign "has not made a discernible difference in the way Exxon is addressing climate change."[16] Perhaps not surprisingly, Engine No. 1 disagrees. The firm has published a report highlighting the many changes that Exxon undertook since the fateful election and arguing that they not only increased shareholder value, but it would have been impossible without the new directors.[17]

Having said that, in my view at least, there is bound to be some impact—for two reasons. First, the new board members bring such differentiated experiences and views that it seems likely they will steer deliberations in a somewhat different direction than the old board would have. Second, and perhaps even more importantly, Engine No. 1's victory was a major surprise to Exxon and many other corporations. It drove hard the message that investors' views matter and that dissatisfied investors may indeed change the course of the company. I would imagine this knowledge will influence many executives and board members.

5.5.2 Green bonds

We've already touched on bonds in this book, for example, when we explained their pricing in Chapter 3, when we discussed predictors of their returns in Chapter 4, or when we considered their potential for impact earlier in this chapter. In all these situations, we referred to "regular" corporate bonds, abstracting from any special modifications or properties they may have. But now, to further illustrate the financing costs channel for impact, we will introduce the increasingly important category of labeled bonds.

The key property of labeled bonds is that the funds a company raises through their issuance are earmarked for specific projects (hence, the "use of proceeds" bonds). The specific label we put on a bond depends on what type of projects the bond finances. For example, a bond earmarked for climate-related projects is usually referred to as a "green bond;" other bonds may be "blue" (if they finance water projects) or "social" (projects with social benefits). In addition, labeled bonds also include another variant, "sustainability-linked bonds." Such bonds make their payment structure (for example, the coupon rate) a function of sustainability-related key performance indicators (KPIs). For example, a company may issue a bond with a coupon payment that depends on the firm's achieving some decarbonization objectives: if the firm manages to do so, it will pay less in interest.

The market for labeled bonds has boomed in recent years, driven by the broad interest in ESG investing on one side, and by firms' issuing securities that cater to this interest on the other. The total amount outstanding in such bonds went from about $300 billion in 2018 to $3.2 trillion in mid-2023.[18] Historically, much of the issuance was in green bonds, although in recent years other types of labeled bonds are quickly catching up and today make up about half of the overall issuance. Moreover, while the first labeled bonds were issued by institutions such as the European Investment Bank or the World Bank, nowadays, this is the domain of corporations and sovereigns, or even municipalities.

Why would investors be interested in these instruments? On the one hand, the answer may seem obvious: these bonds allow investors to finance the specific activities investors care about. It would seem natural for a climate investor to hold green bonds. On the other hand, while a green bond may finance green projects, it may be issued by a company that also has brown projects that it finances from other sources. In fact, most issuers, corporate or sovereign, issue both labeled and "regular" bonds, frequently at the same time. The proceeds from the issuance of regular bonds have general use and could finance projects that a sustainable investor might disapprove of. Perhaps all green projects of that issuer will then be financed by green bonds, and whatever not-so-green projects remain will be financed by regular bonds. In such a case, the more a company issues green bonds, the browner its remaining bonds become, and the overall sustainability profile of the company does not change.

Luckily, there is a powerful argument that labeled bonds do matter and that companies issuing them have an incentive to undertake relatively more sustainable projects. This argument centers on impact and relies on a phenomenon known as greenium. Greenium is based on a comparison of otherwise similar labeled and regular bonds, issued by the same issuer. The idea is that ESG-motivated investors are willing to pay a premium for labeled bonds relative to ordinary bonds. As we saw in Chapter 3, the higher the price of a bond, the lower the yield that bond has.

Greenium is then defined as the difference between ordinary and green bond yields. If ESG-motivated investors accept relatively lower yields on green bonds, then this means that they are willing to provide the company with cheaper capital, as long as that capital is used for appropriate (say, green) projects.

Think about a company that used to issue only regular, unlabeled bonds. That firm has a certain cost of financing, which reflects the views of all its investors, sustainable and not. The cost of capital features in the firm's capital budgeting process and is used to select corporate investment projects. Projects that have a positive net present value (NPV) when assessed using that cost of capital, get undertaken; projects with a negative NPV, do not. Now, suppose this firm changes the structure of its issuance and decides to issue both green and regular bonds. With greenium, green bonds reflect the cost of financing that is cheaper than before. This means that when we assess green projects at this lower cost of capital, more projects will have positive NPV than before. Conversely, if the yield on regular bonds rises (now that "regular" capital is provided predominantly by non-ESG investors), fewer brown projects have a positive NPV. In consequence, the firm shifts its corporate investment activity, undertaking more green and fewer brown projects than it used to. This is the exact type of impact that sustainable investors are interested in. The argument holds not just for green bonds but also for other (social, blue, etc.) types of labeled bonds. It is perhaps even clearer for sustainability-linked bonds. For example, such a bond may make the coupon payment dependent on the firm achieving a decarbonization target. If the firm succeeds, it will then pay strictly less to service its debt, which gives it a clear economic incentive to decarbonize.

Crucially, the channel of impact is clearly the cost of financing. Green, social, or sustainability-linked bonds do not confer any control rights on the investor. Some might say that the fact that these bonds proceeds are earmarked to specific projects is a form of control. I disagree. This is just a way for the firm to secure cheaper financing than it would otherwise. For example, take the sustainability-linked bond I mentioned earlier. The firm will decide whether to meet its KPIs based on an economic calculation. If the cost of its reaching the decarbonization target is low enough, or if the financing costs are sufficiently attractive, then the firm will make efforts to reach the goal. If not, then the firm will forego that cheaper financing. So, there is a potential impact, but it depends on the firm's cost of capital calculations, and not on the holders of sustainability-linked bonds having some form of control over the firm's activities.

Since the potential impact of labeled bonds depends on greenium, we should discuss how large greenium is in practice. In my view, there is some, but it is typically relatively low. There is a good reason for that: bond markets correctly view labeled and ordinary bonds as close substitutes (they are, after all, issued by the same issuers). When otherwise similar labeled and regular bonds trade at markedly different prices (which must be the case if they have different yields), at least some investors will try to capitalize on it. The trade is to "sell high and buy low," which in this case would mean trying to short the more expensive labeled bond, while at the same time buying the cheaper regular bond, ideally matching the two bonds maturity, seniority, etc. This trade may not always be frictionless, since short selling involves extra costs (more on this in the next chapter), there may be liquidity issues, etc.—but it is reasonable to expect that when the price discrepancy is particularly large, investors will have more economic incentive to step in.

Having said that, some academic studies indeed have found evidence of a modest amount of greenium. For example, an early study of US municipal green and ordinary bonds found that the former had yields lower by about 6 basis points (i.e., 0.06%).[19]

Other papers look at sovereign issuers. Here too, there is evidence of a small amount of greenium. For example, the German government has been issuing twin green and ordinary bonds since 2020, and an analysis of these bonds suggests that greenium changes over time, but tends to be in low basis points (perhaps 2–7 basis points, or 0.02–0.07%).[20]

Are these differences in yields meaningful? I would argue that they are, although we should not overstate them. Once you multiply the small difference in yields by a large amount of issuance, you could arrive at economically large quantities. For example, the issuance of labeled bonds in 2023 was estimated at about $900 billion.[21] Assuming a greenium of 5 basis points (0.05%), this corresponds to financing costs that are lower by $450 million than they would have been should the same amount of capital be raised through ordinary bonds. These cost savings matter, although probably only on the margin. There are surely some, but probably not too many, investment projects that go from negative to positive NPV when the cost of capital changes by 0.05%. This is perhaps reflected in the volume of issuance, which tends to be meaningfully higher for ordinary than for labeled bonds (for example, in the case of the German bonds we mentioned above, the issuance of ordinary bonds was five times higher than that of green bonds). To me, the bottom line is that labeled bonds have impact, through the financing cost channel, and that they will be critically important for some corporate projects—but given the volumes and the greenium we see today, they are perhaps unlikely to lead to wholesome changes in the overall economy.

5.5.3 Building net zero portfolios

In our last example, we will discuss net zero pledges. This increasingly important initiative is motivated by investors' desire to help transition the global economy to net zero carbon emissions. As per its second progress report, published in October 2023, the Net-Zero Asset Owner Alliance counts 86 members, collectively managing $9.5 trillion in assets. To assess the potential and actual impact of these assets, we need to ask how these investors' portfolio decisions can incentivize portfolio companies to decarbonize.

For net-zero investors, a key driver of their allocations is the carbon footprint of their portfolio. As we saw in Chapter 4, carbon footprinting apportions the greenhouse gas emissions of portfolio companies to their investors, prorating emissions based on each investor's fractional ownership, usually reflecting both equity and bonds. The net-zero investment goal is then to control the carbon footprint of one's portfolio and to gradually reduce it, typically along a predefined glide path. This makes a lot of sense, at least when the composition of the portfolio is held constant. This is because when we hold a fixed stake in each company, we can only reduce our carbon footprint when our portfolio companies start to emit less. Investors then have a clear incentive to utilize all the control tools they have, engage with the company and vote proxies, to entice the firm to decarbonize even faster.

Unfortunately, it is unrealistic to expect that the portfolio composition will remain unchanged. In practice, reducing the portfolio ownership in the heaviest emitters is much easier than persuading portfolio companies to cut their emissions. Not surprisingly, most net zero investors primarily rely on this easier option to achieve their portfolio decarbonization goals. To be clear, these investors undoubtedly vote proxies and engage with their portfolio companies, but they do so already after they formed their green, low carbon portfolios.

So, we can expect net-zero investors to gradually reduce their ownership of heavy emitters and instead tilt toward relatively greener companies. We know from our earlier discussion that doing so affects the channels of impact. When it comes to the heavy emitters, net-zero portfolios will increasingly sell them, reducing their ability to use the control channel: you cannot vote or meaningfully engage with a company you no longer hold. This portfolio decision will, however, put increasing pressure on the price of the heavy emitters and potentially influence them through the financing costs channel. At the same time, net zero investors will tilt their portfolios toward green companies and will be able to increasingly affect them through both channels of impact.

This shift in influence is rather unfortunate. As we already noted, investors tend to prefer the control channel of impact. They cannot exercise it for the companies that matter much more for what the investors care about: global greenhouse gas emissions. They do have more control over green companies, and will likely vote and engage with them. However, the outcome of these engagements may not matter much for global emissions, because, as we saw in Chapter 4, these green companies only account for a small fraction of global emissions.

But not all is lost. As we discussed, portfolio choices have an impact via the cost of capital channel. So, it is possible that net-zero investors, together with other investors who share similar ESG portfolio goals, may still have some influence over the heavy emitters. It turns out that there is more and more evidence that such impact actually occurs. For example, an interesting recent study went straight to the source and investigated how companies themselves view their own cost of capital.[22] The study sifted through earnings call transcripts to identify instances where the company reported their financing cost assumptions to their investors. The key finding is that before 2016, there was no apparent difference in the perceived cost of capital between brown and green firms. However, after 2016, brown firms reported financing costs that were 2.6 percentage points higher than their greener peers. This is a large difference, likely to influence firm investment decisions. It may be impossible to prove that it was driven by changes in ESG investors' portfolio decisions since 2016, but I would conjecture that this accounts for at least some of the effect.

In addition, there are a variety of industry reports that support this conclusion. To choose just one example, a recent analysis compared the financing costs for various energy-related businesses.[23] The analysis showed that the difference in the cost of capital for offshore oil and renewable energy has been steadily increasing over the prior few years, growing from about 5–10% in 2010 to above 15% in 2020. Over the same period, the cost of capital for natural gas went from below that of renewables to over 5% more expensive. Again, I would ascribe this change at least partially to the collective actions of ESG investors.[24] We can also directly ask the affected companies. For example, respondents to the Q4 2021 Dallas Fed Energy Survey commented that "Service companies have very little access to new capital, and cash reserves are being exhausted" or "Constrained capital will lead to significantly higher commodity prices. And it isn't the administration's fault—this is a Wall Street and environmental, social and governance-led charge."

Overall, the impact of net-zero investors is shifting toward the financing costs channel. On the one hand, this may worry these investors, given that this not their preferred channel of influence. On the other hand, this channel seems to have clear impact, so it might deserve more recognition than it currently gets.

Notes

1. For example, Agrawal, A., Jaffe, J.F., and Mandelker, G.N. (1992). The post-merger performance of acquiring firms: a

re-examination of an anomaly. *Journal of Finance*, 47 (4): 1605–1621 report that "stockholders of acquiring firms suffer a statistically significant loss of about 10% over the five-year post-merger period."

2. Burrough, B. and Helyar, J. (2005). *Barbarians at the Gate. The Fall of RJR Nabisco*. Harper Business Essentials.

3. The example is adapted from Hart, O. and Zingales, L. (2017). Companies should maximize shareholder welfare not market value. *Journal of Law, Finance, and Accounting*, 2 (2): 247–274; https://scholar.harvard.edu/files/hart/files/108.00000022-hart-vol2no2-jlfa-0022_002.pdf. See this paper for a longer discussion about maximizing shareholder value and its alternatives.

4. Friedman, M. (1970). The social responsibility of business is to increase its profits. *New York Times Magazine*, 13 September: 32–33, 122–124.

5. We keep on trying though. For example, some companies may seek the "B corporation" status that aims to address a firm's social and environmental externalities. As another example, the Hart and Zingales paper (n. iii in this chapter) proposes maximizing shareholder welfare rather than shareholder value.

6. As per Aviva website, https://www.avivainvestors.com/en-gb/capabilities/regulatory/voting-rights-strategy/

7. See Flammer, C. (2015). Does corporate social responsibility lead to superior financial performance? A regression discontinuity approach. *Management Science*, 61 (11): 2549–2568.

8. Specifically, Blackrock says it had "3,880+ total engagements" with "2,580+ unique companies engaged." Source: https://www.blackrock.com/corporate/literature/publication/annual-stewardship-report-2022.pdf

9. See, for example Brav, A., Jiang, W., and Kim, H. (2010). Hedge fund activism: a review. *Foundations and Trends in*

Finance, 4 (3): 1–66. The evidence was also replicated in Fos, V. (2016). The disciplinary effects of proxy contests. *Management Science*, 63 (3).

10. Bebchuk, L.A., Brav, A., and Jiang, W. (2015). The long-term effects of hedge fund activism. *Columbia Law Review*, 115: 1085–1156.

11. Brav et al. (2010). see note ix, this chapter.

12. Dimson, E., Karakas, O., and Li, X. (2015). Active owner-ship. *Review of Financial Studies*, 28 (12): 3225–3268.

13. For a discussion of how sustainability may increase firm value, you may want to consult the wonderfully titled book by Edmans, A. (2020). *Grow the Pie: How Great Companies Deliver Both Purpose and Profit*. Cambridge University Press.

14. For a longer discussion of these issues, see Jones, B., Men-delson, M.A., and Pomorski, L. (2023). How portfolios can impact the real economy. AQR paper.

15. "135 investors managing more than $2 trillion are form-ing a coalition to push Exxon Mobil Corp into making sweeping changes including refreshing its board and focus-ing more on energy transition." Herbst-Bayliss, S. (2021, 29 January). Shareholders create coalition to pressure Exxon for change. Reuters

16. Sorkin, A.R., Mattu, R., Warner, B., et al. (2023, 31 May). Reassessing the board fight that was meant to transform Exxon. *The New York Times*.

17. See https://engine1.com/transforming/articles/exxon-mobil-one-year-later/

18. MSCI. (2023, 31 August). Labeled bonds quarterly market overview Q2 2023. https://www.msci.com/www/research-report/labeled-bonds-quarterly-market/04033036183#:~:text=The%20market%20added%20USD%20172,the%20end%20of%20the%20quarter

19. Baker, M., Bergstresser, D., Serafeim, G., and Wurgler, J. (2018). Financing the response to climate change: the pricing and ownership of U.S. green bonds," NBER working paper 25194. Greenium in the municipal market is a contentious topic though, Larker, D.F. and Watts, E.M. (2020). found little evidence of it in Where's the greenium? *Journal of Accounting and Economics*, 69 (2–3).

20. Pastor, L., Stambaugh, R.F., and Taylor, L.A. (2022). Dissecting green returns. *Journal of Financial Economics*, 146 (2): 403–424.

21. S&P Global report, https://www.spglobal.com/esg/insights/featured/special-editorial/global-sustainable-bonds-2023-issuance-to-exceed-900-billion

22. Gormsen, N.J., Huber, K., and Oh, S. (2023). Climate capitalists. University of Chicago working paper.

23. Goldman Sachs. (2020, 16 June). Carbonomics: the green engine of economic recovery. Goldman Sachs Equity Research.

24. Additional evidence can be found in McKinsey (2021). Why ESG is here to stay; Institutional Asset Manager (2021, 15 August). ESG concerns rapidly increasing cost of capital for oil companies, says Aegon Asset Management; or Gas Outlook (2022, 27 January). Is ESG really starving the oil and gas industry of capital?

Chapter 6

Sustainability beyond Traditional Strategies

S o far, our discussion has focused primarily on stocks and bonds. It should not end there, though. ESG investors increasingly think about sustainability in the context of their broader portfolio, which may also include allocations to alternative asset classes. Historically, such allocations were usually omitted from sustainability discussions. There is nothing surprising about that. Investors started with more intuitive traditional asset classes that, in any case, tend to account for the majority of their allocations. Over the years or perhaps even decades, the investment community has reached at least some consensus about ESG integration, voting, and engagement that come with traditional equity and bond mandates. Now their attention is shifting to other strategies. In part, this is also driven by their end clients and even the regulators, who are more vocal nowadays that sustainability claims and reporting should reflect investors' overall allocations.

Luckily for us, the foundation we set in the earlier chapters holds not just for traditional equity or bonds, but also more broadly for other investments. Admittedly, there are nuances that we need to control for, but with all the tools we've already acquired, we should be ready for that challenge. In fact, we already allowed for some asset-class-specific nuances earlier in this book, for example, when discussing corporate bonds and how different they may be compared to equity (for example, when it comes to impact, in Chapter 5).

In this chapter, we will move beyond traditional asset classes and will discuss alternative strategies, starting with shorting. We will also tackle financial derivatives, especially those that give investors exposure to commodity prices. In both cases, we will revisit the basic questions we wrestled with in earlier chapters: we will ask whether ESG can help us identify risks and return opportunities in a given asset class, and whether investors can impact real economic decisions by investing in that asset class.

6.1   Shorting

In this section, we discuss hedge fund-type strategies, which are able to both buy (go long) and short stocks and bonds. We already know how to deal with long positions—we discussed these at length so far in this book. But how can we handle the short side of a hedge fund's portfolio, and could we even say anything about the net exposure (longs minus shorts) that such a fund may have?

To start with, let's make sure that we all know and agree on what short selling is. Conceptually, it is a way to implement an investment view that an asset (stock, bond, or any other security) is likely to go down in price. If we happen to hold this asset (in the jargon, if we are to long the asset), then we would act on the view by selling the security. But what if we do not hold that security anymore? This is where shorting comes in. There is a way for us to sell the asset we do not hold—we can "short sell it" or simply "short it." The idea of selling something you do not own may seem jarring, and I imagine that is why shorting is often spoken of with distrust or even contempt. This is unfortunate because, in practice, shorting is more prosaic than some commentators imagine it to be, and in my view, it does not deserve its somewhat nefarious reputation.

So how can you sell something you do not own, say a stock that is not in your portfolio? The answer is that you need to borrow it first.[1] You would typically do this through a broker, who would identify (locate) an institution that owns that stock today and is not planning to sell it in the near future. Such an institution may be a pension fund that owns the stock, perhaps in its passive equity allocation, and thus will, in principle, be prepared to hold it for as long as it is in the market index. The pension fund may then be willing to lend the stock to you. It will expect to earn a fee for this service, and the size of the fee will be driven by market competition. The lending fee tends to be larger for stocks that are held by few institutions or those that are in high demand by short sellers.

Once we borrow the stock, we turn around and sell it in the market. Very importantly, the pension fund that lent us the stock still has a claim on it—not directly, but through the IOU that we gave it when borrowing the stock. This means that if the stock pays a dividend, we need to pay the pension fund that amount. Moreover, at some point, we will need to return the stock to the pension fund. This may be because we want to close the transaction (perhaps the price dropped to the level we expected) but also because the pension fund may recall the loan. At that time, we will need to purchase the stock at the prevailing price and then return it to the pension fund. With that, our short-selling transaction is completed. We made a profit if the price we sold the stock at the outset is larger than the price we bought it back to conclude the transaction (after accounting for the lending fees, dividends we owed to the pension fund, etc.). This will happen if the price of the stock falls, and the more it decreases, the larger the short seller's profit. Conversely, if the price goes up, then we bought the stock at a higher price than we had sold it at, and we realize an investment loss on the transaction.

Now that we understand the basics of short selling, let's consider the various ways sustainability may be important for this type of transaction. We will cast our analysis in terms of climate to make it more concrete and to highlight specific examples. Moreover, the potential benefits of shorting are perhaps clearest for managing sustainability-type risks, and such risks are more apparent for climate than for many other ESG issues. Having said that, the arguments we overview in the following sub-sections apply to most other facets of ESG as well. The only exception, which we will discuss at the end of the section, is when the investor has ethical reasons to avoid particular sources of investment return.

As with bonds, we will discuss three broad reasons why sustainable investors should consider shorting: hedging ESG-type risks, producing risk-adjusted returns (also known as "alpha"), and impact. As you may already guess, the bottom line will be that shorting can be very helpful in the pursuit of the first two goals, and there is a good argument that it could even incrementally enhance investors' ability to have impact. Before we arrive at these conclusions, please allow me an important caveat: shorting is not for everybody. On the one hand, the view that shorting is nefarious does not survive closer scrutiny. On the other, it is an "alternative" investment technique for a reason, and requires relatively more experience and better monitoring etc. systems. It is also costly, as we saw in the description of its mechanics above. Having said that, I do believe that there is a place for shorting in a sustainable investor's toolbox, and as we will see below, there are sophisticated investors who are vocal proponents of shorting.

6.1.1   Managing risks with short sales

Many investors decide to manage climate risks in their investment portfolios. A recent example can be the net zero pledge signed by Oregon's Treasurer and the Oregon Investment Council.[2] The pledge is to gradually reduce the carbon emissions in the State of Oregon's investment portfolio. While many net-zero pledges reflect investors' desire to have an impact, Oregon's was explicitly linked to financial climate risks. The idea is that as the investment portfolio reduces its holdings of carbon-heavy, "brown" assets, the resulting exposure to climate-type risks will also decrease.

To begin with, let's note that Oregon is not unique. Risk is consistently listed as one of the key reasons why asset owners care about climate.[3] Many other investors have similar investment views and also aim to underweight or simply not hold stocks or other securities deemed to have high climate risk. The resulting portfolios will have relatively less exposure than before, and perhaps also less exposure than the overall market or a specific benchmark index that the investor cares about. But there's a limit. It is unlikely, and maybe even outright impossible, that the investor will be able to eliminate any and all exposure to these risks. They are simply too pervasive. Even a green, low-carbon stock will typically have *some* emissions, not to mention potential indirect climate risks of the type we discussed at the end of Chapter 4. It is true that a few stocks may come with negative climate risk exposure. Such stocks may be expected to do particularly well when climate risks arise, perhaps because they produce goods and services that are in demand at such times. But it is unlikely there are very many such stocks, meaning that a portfolio concentrated in them is likely to be rather under-diversified.

There is an analogy between the situation we are describing and other pervasive, systemic risks. For example, take the risk of the equity market overall. An individual stock's exposure to this risk, usually referred to as the stock's beta, measures how much a stock comoves with the overall market. Not surprisingly, most stocks have positive betas, meaning they can be expected to go up when the market overall goes up, and fall when the market overall falls. It is not too difficult to find stocks with less exposure than the overall market (technically, beta lower than one), and many asset owners indeed have large mandates focusing on low-beta stocks. However, these mandates still have meaningful market risk exposure. They give you less equity risk—perhaps 60% of the typical stock's beta—but on average, you still tend to go up and down with the broad equity market. And yes, you may be able to find stocks that have roughly zero betas (their movements are uncorrelated with those of the broader market) or maybe even stocks with negative betas (which might give you valuable insurance against market movements). But there aren't many such stocks—perhaps ironically, a low-risk allocation that concentrates on such few extremely low beta stocks will be very under-diversified.

Enter shorting. Whether we want to manage climate risks or non-ESG risks such as equity risk, shorting will typically allow us much more flexibility than we could attain in a traditional, long-only allocation. This is because shorting reverses the sign of a stock's exposure, allowing us to turn highly exposed stocks into climate insurance. To see this, consider a very brown firm— perhaps an oil major that is uninterested in transitioning to green energy, or a utility that is powered exclusively by coal. Such companies are exposed to a wide variety of climate risks: for example, their clients may shift to renewable energy, governments may impose a tax on carbon emissions, etc. If we long the brown stock and such a risk occurs, then the value of our investment decreases. However, if we short the stock, we are positioned to gain from a decline in price. If a climate risk transpires and meaningfully reduces the value of the stock, then our short position makes money. Thinking back to the mechanics of shorting we described above, we could then buy the stock back at a lower price than we originally sold it at, leaving us with an investment gain. The more extreme the climate risk, and the deeper the drop in the value of the brown firm, the more profit we make on the short position.

This is a very attractive feature for risk-averse climate investors. For better or worse, there are many more stocks that have high climate exposure than there are stocks that are clear green solutions. So, the investor may be able to build a diversified collection of such high-exposure stocks and short them. Another major advantage of this approach is that by shorting particularly brown stocks, the investor may be able to tolerate purchases of brown, but not quite-as-brown stocks in a similar industry.

For example, it may be difficult for a traditional mandate to remove most of the climate risk, let alone approach net zero, and still hold a meaningful position in, say, the Energy sector.[4] This is because most, if not all, stocks in that specific sector likely have a meaningful climate risk exposure, otherwise they would not be in that sector in the first place. This is unfortunate because the investor may otherwise see attractive opportunities in the sector. Shorting changes the situation. The investor may want to short Energy firms with the most meaningful climate exposure and buy (long) less climate-exposed Energy companies. The investor may even decide to have a meaningful long position in Energy overall, but neutralize climate risks at the same time.

As an important aside, to effectively manage climate risk, investors need to articulate how they would measure such risk. Investors may wish to incorporate some of the industry-standard measures, including those we discussed in Chapter 4 (e.g., Scope 1+2 emissions intensity) or any number of new measures proposed in this space (e.g., the supply chain metric we introduced in Chapter 4, but also climate VaRs, Implied Temperature Rise scores, etc.).

Finally, as I mentioned earlier, shorting has a difficult reputation, and many commentators are (in my view, unfortunately) distrustful or outright critical of it. But if there is one role of shorting that attracts less criticism, it is risk management. The case for shorting in that context is just too strong. We will soon see that one can also build a strong ESG risk management case for derivatives and for commodity derivatives in particular. And, as I alluded to earlier, the case is broader than just ESG. Think back to my point that it is effectively impossible to build a traditional equity allocation with no exposure to equity risk. This, too, changes with shorting. Portfolio managers can balance their long and short beta exposures to build an equity market-neutral portfolio or to deliberately target a level of beta that may be difficult to attain in a long-only allocation. (As it turns out, you may also choose to hedge out the equity risk of your portfolio using derivatives.)

6.1.2   Implementing alpha views with shorting

Some investors use climate information and their predictions for weather trends, policy responses, etc. to arrive at return (aka alpha) views. For example, they may try to identify the "green solutions" we mentioned earlier. The investor may invest in such stocks in the hope of making an investment profit, especially if they expect the economy to decarbonize, the regulators to pass climate-friendly regulations, etc. Could shorting help in incorporating such investment views into one's portfolio? You won't be surprised that the answer is yes. Most obviously, shorting can help the investor act on negative views about a given stock. In a traditional strategy, the most the investor could do is not hold such stocks. But if the investor has confidence in the investment view, then the best way to take advantage of the information may well be to short the brown stock outright. As we saw above, this will allow the investor to capitalize on the subsequent fall in price—not just to avoid an investment loss in the traditional strategy but to make a potential profit in a mandate that allows shorting.

In fact, I would argue that historically ESG has been associated with "short" rather than "long" investment ideas. Speakers at ESG conferences often talk about sustainability as a source of investment insights, and, at least until recently, these conversations focused on downside rather than upside potential. For example, ESG was a way to identify poorly managed stocks, stocks at the brink of an environmental controversy, a labor dispute, etc. Climate conversations were heavy on stranded assets that the market underappreciates, overpricing the companies that hold such assets on their balance sheets. In all these situations, the way to incorporate the investment view is not just to divest the stock in question, but also to actually short it.

Admittedly, conference conversations in the last few years have shifted toward green solutions. It turns out that even here shorting can help the investor build such a view into a portfolio. Shorting can lead to better risk management that allows the investor to purchase more of the green solution than the investor would otherwise have. To see this, suppose the investor identifies an oil major that is heavily investing in green technology and that has a plausible plan to transition in that direction. There may be great upside potential for such a stock. At the same time, the investor who buys the stock also assumes a position in the Oil & Gas industry, in the country where the firm resides, etc. Moreover, the investor risks that the green transition may come later than expected. All these risks may curb the investor's appetite and limit the maximum position they will allow in the stock. However, if the investor is able to short, they may be able to buy the transitioning oil company while at the same time shorting another oil firm, perhaps even in the same country, that refuses to engage on climate and diversify their production. This way, the investor may be able to capitalize on both ends of their investment view, while at the same time hedging industry, country, or even climate risks by carefully sizing their long and short positions.

6.1.3 Seeking impact with shorting

Finally, a very important motivation for climate-oriented investors is impact. As we saw in Chapter 5, impact is the desire to use one's portfolio to affect real-economy outcomes, for example, corporate greenhouse gas emissions.

The potential impact of shorts is a divisive and hotly debated topic. I have had ample opportunity to experience it through my service on industry working groups and committees discussing shorting and derivatives and through presenting my work at seminars and conferences. This puts me in a good position to discuss the topic and hopefully identify at least some reasons for the discord among the investment community.

First, let us leverage the framework we developed in Chapter 5 and ask why shorting might have any impact in the first place. Of the two channels of influence, control and financing costs, only the latter is applicable for shorting. This is because shorting does not give the investor any decision rights. They do not get a vote at the shareholder meeting (and are likely less than welcome there in the first place). Shorters also do not engage directly with their portfolio companies. It's not that they have nothing to say, but the economic incentives complicate any such engagement. Shorts benefit from a drop in the price of the company they short, so it is difficult to see how they could fruitfully communicate with corporate management.

But while control only accrues to long positions, impact via financing costs is more general. As we discussed in Chapter 5, any portfolio decision has the potential to influence stock or bond prices and thus also affect a company's cost of capital. Purchases might increase the price and lower the expected cost of financing, while sales (whether traditional or short sales) might decrease the price and increase financing costs.

This distinction is not just important on its own but also helps address a major misconception in industry discussions of impact and shorting. The misconception arises from a seemingly natural question: do shorts have more impact than longs? We now have the tools to address this question. Assuming you are buying or shorting the same notional amount, the impact on price and financing costs is likely similar for longs and shorts. But, importantly, going long on some securities may also give you a control right, for example, a vote, that you never get with shorting. So, in a head-to-head comparison, of course, going long with a stock has a larger plausible impact than shorting a similar amount of the same stock may have.

Unfortunately, directly comparing longs and shorts on the same security is irrelevant. The point is that it is exceedingly unlikely that a sustainable investor will choose between buying a stock or shorting that same stock. If the investor likes the stock, whether for impact or return reasons, they will then buy the stock. But if the investor dislikes the stock, then they are highly unlikely to buy it. They may sell the stock and perhaps fully divest it—or they could potentially short it.

So, in practice, the right question to ask is whether shorting could have more impact than divestment. For a realistic illustration, let's come back to the net-zero climate investor we considered in Chapter 5. The investor wants to build a green portfolio, so they would naturally focus their purchases on low-carbon companies, companies that produce green economy-related goods and services, etc. Such investors would very rarely consider buying companies on the opposite, brown, end of the spectrum. They will divest them instead. As we saw in Chapter 5, investors in this space often want their financial allocations to have impact and, at least at the margin, incentivize their portfolio companies to transition toward low carbon. And the good news is that, as we saw, there is evidence that divestment indeed has impact, through the financing costs channel.

Could such a green investor increase his or her impact if they also allow shorting? I argue that they would, again because of the influence on financing costs. In this context, shorting is simply a continuation of divestment. Divestment means that investors sell until their holdings reach zero. Shorting means that you keep selling past that point and quite literally acquire a negative holding of the security (remember that a short seller's profits are the negative of those of a long position). So, if divestment has impact, then so does shorting, because it relies on the same economic mechanism—the selling pressure which will eventually translate into lower prices.

The intuition above notwithstanding, is there any empirical evidence that shorts may indeed have impact? It turns out there is. In Chapter 5, we already discussed academic research that shows that investors' portfolio decisions influence companies' cost of capital, and we can again appeal to this evidence here. But there are also papers that directly assess whether shorting influences firms' real-economy activities. One such paper leverages a "quasi-natural experiment," where regulation constrained investors from shorting some stocks, while allowing them to short other firms.[5] By comparing the activities of the two groups of firms, the researchers documented that short-selling led to decreases in stock prices, consistent with our earlier discussion. More interestingly, they also saw a reduction in equity issuance and investment, which again aligns well with the financing costs channel of impact. Higher financing costs make issuance relatively less attractive for the firm. They also mean that fewer corporate investment projects will have positive NPV (since we are discounting their future cashflows at a higher rate), which would explain the drop in firms' real investment. While these effects were stronger in relatively small firms, they confirm that shorting can indeed influence real-economy corporate decisions.

At this point, you might see something to the argument that shorts have impact. But if you need additional convincing, consider asking a corporate executive if they care about shorts. Chances are they do, and they probably dislike the practice. This opens up another role for shorting: signaling to the management that some investors disagree with their actions, or with the direction their company has taken. I would not go as far as calling this "engagement." As we discussed above, there is no plausible engagement with shorts. But knowing that their company has a large short interest, or that it is increasingly difficult to borrow the company's stock because many investors want to short it, could be a way to get the management to start paying more attention—which is more than divestment could do.

Finally, shorting may also allow investors to have more impact with the stocks investors buy. This is a variant of the argument we saw before: shorting helps investors better manage their portfolio risks. We can reuse our earlier example of a long–short manager who chooses to build longs in those climate-intensive firms that are transitioning well, that have larger green revenues, etc., while shorting climate-intensive laggards. The resulting allocation could generate meaningful engagement opportunities with at least some of the companies that have a large climate impact. In contrast, a long-only portfolio subject to the same climate risk considerations may not be able to hold any such companies.

6.1.4   Sustainability reporting with short positions

The last topic we will cover is sustainability reporting with short positions. Reporting may sound boring, but this topic becomes surprisingly exciting and hotly debated once you add short positions to the picture. Part of the reason is that reporting is no longer optional: many asset owners, and sometimes even regulators, require investors to produce sustainability reports for all their strategies and portfolios. For most investors, such reporting is already standard for traditional strategies, and it is increasingly difficult to argue that alternative strategies are out of scope. One of the goals of reporting is to give investors a better understanding of their portfolio risks, including, say, climate risks. If we agree that such risks are relevant for traditional assets, it should be obvious that they may also be relevant for alternatives such as hedge funds, with their long–short portfolios. So, if a pension plan only publishes climate reports for the former but not for the latter, then its stakeholders arguably have only a partial understanding of the overall climate exposure of the plan's total investment portfolio.

This means that if the goal of reporting is to present investors with a holistic view of an allocation, reporting should include not just longs, but also shorts. Most investors will not see anything wrong with reporting longs and shorts separately, on the standalone basis. The big question, and the reason why investors vehemently disagree about what the "right" solution is, is whether it is fine to net out shorts against longs.

As usual, this question will be the least controversial for sustainability risks. For example, if you are buying companies with a large climate risk exposure while at the same shorting companies with a similarly large climate exposure, it is OK to claim that your long–short portfolio overall hedges out climate risk. Most practitioners would agree that it is perfectly acceptable to do so. We might quibble about the way we measure the climate exposure of any one stock (as we saw in Chapter 4, this is a formidable challenge), but once we agree on the measure, it should allow netting longs and shorts. This is the case with any other source of risk. For example, overall market exposure, measured by beta, does net out between longs and shorts, which is why many hedge fund portfolios are referred to as "equity market neutral." You could build a long–short portfolio that nets out the exposure to countries, currencies, or interest rates, all by matching the exposure of the long and the short book. There is no reason why sustainability risks should be any different.

The argument becomes more difficult when we consider other reasons for reporting sustainability portfolio characteristics. For example, investors interested in impact sometimes claim that only long exposures count for that purpose. As we saw in Chapter 5, this view reflects only one of the two channels for impact, control. And indeed, if sustainable reporting is meant to reflect impact through the control channel, then shorts do not count. However, this seems like a rather narrow use case for reporting, and I have not yet heard of any investor who would express a need for something that specific. But I cannot deny that such an investor may exist. Luckily, the best practice I outlined earlier, reporting both longs and shorts and, if the manager deems it appropriate, also the net position, seems to achieve the investor's goal. They would simply take the long position from the report and ignore the short and net figures. Of course, if an investor wanted more precision specifically for the control channel, you would want to design a report that not only excludes shorts, but also excludes those longs that may no longer have a vote. This may happen because some long positions may be synthetic or derivatives-based but also because, ironically, many long investors may lend out their shares to short sellers.

Another important use case for reporting is to assess an investor's involvement in sustainable, or not sustainable, activities. A classic case here is carbon footprinting, or assessing how much of a company's greenhouse gas emissions are "financed" through an investor's stake in the company. As a reminder from Chapter 4, if a company emits 50 million tons of CO_2 and an investor holds 5% of that company in their portfolio, then this investor's carbon footprint from that company is 5% of 50 or 2.5 million tons of CO_2. This intuitive calculation becomes meaningfully less simple when we consider shorting. The issue here is again whether one can net out the carbon financed by longs and the carbon implied in short positions.[6] Such netting seems deeply counterintuitive at first blush. However, it is not so easy to come up with hard arguments why it is wrong. The common argument one hears is that shorting does not remove any carbon from the atmosphere. That is undoubtedly true, but also irrelevant to this question. Shorting does not remove carbon, but neither does going long cause firms to emit more. We are just trying to apportion the real economy emissions, whatever they are, to the financial stake investors may have in the underlying company.

I could provide a few different arguments as to why netting longs and shorts is not just acceptable but outright critical for the accounting to make sense—for example, without it, the carbon footprint summed across all market participants would not be equal to actual real economy emissions. This may be interesting but is unlikely to change the minds of investors who are already skeptical about shorting in the first place. Instead, I prefer to address the issue by moving away from the usual context of an individual mandate ("what is the carbon footprint of this hedge fund") and posing it in the context of an investor's overall allocation ("what is the carbon footprint of this pension fund's overall equity program"). For most asset owners, the long book is much larger than the short book, and the allocator may be net long overall even if they allow limited shorting in some mandates. For example, a pension fund may hold $10 million in shares of an oil major in a long-only mandate, say in their passive allocation to equity markets. At the same time, the pension fund may have a hedge fund program that shorts $1 million worth of stock of the same issuer. You might balk at a scenario in which the same asset owner is both long and short the same company in their overall portfolio, but for better or worse this is a realistic case. This happens in practice because allocators' different mandates often do not speak to each other, if only because they may be managed by different external managers. Our pension fund will then need to decide whether their overall carbon exposure from holding the oil major should be based on the $10 million long position, or on the $9 million short position. (At some point, some commentators suggested we should gross up both longs and shorts and assess the carbon footprint based on the hypothetical $11 million holdings of that firm. That proposal is rather difficult to defend, so not surprisingly investors rarely talk about it anymore.)

You can resolve the reporting controversy for yourself by answering that question. If you answered $10 million, then clearly you believe the pension fund should only focus on the long position, and ignore the shorts. I may not agree, but I accept your view. However, many investors who think about this stylized example allow that when a fund buys $10 million, and (short) sells $1 million of the same security in another mandate, then the fund's economic exposure is only $9 million, and this is what should count toward the fund's carbon footprint. I take it as a win because, as I explained above, many large institutions that allow shorts are still net long overall. In any case, I stand by my recommendation that reporting, including for carbon, should provide investors with separate figures for longs, shorts, and, yes, net. This will get us all the information we need, even if we disagree on how to treat shorts for these purposes.

6.1.5 *Final thoughts on shorting*

To round up our discussion of shorting, it is worth noting that it is also important for an interesting sub-class of traditional strategies that are usually referred to as "130/30" (or extensions, or relaxed constraint strategies). These strategies behave much like traditional equity strategies and still give the investor access to the broad stock market, but they also allow some limited shorting. The short positions lead to more exposure (for every dollar invested, a 130/30 portfolio is able to buy $1.30, while shorting $0.30 worth of stocks), making a more potent, higher-octane strategy. Shorting also allows portfolio managers to better translate their investment views into the portfolio and to better risk manage the portfolio. These strategies were briefly popular in the mid-2000s, but have fallen out of favor until about now.[7] As the interest in the strategies grows, so does the importance of understanding what ESG means for a 130/30 allocation.

As the final note on this topic, as you saw, I believe that shorting can be an important tool for sustainable investors. However, that's not to say that shorting must always and everywhere be part of the solution. For example, some investors apply ESG restrictions because they consider certain businesses unethical or at odds with their belief systems, and they simply do not want to earn any profits from trading such businesses. It seems natural that such investors may refuse any profits from either buying or (short) selling the securities in question. One might argue that capitalizing on a price drop is fundamentally different from earning returns on a long position, but that may be too cute of an argument. In my experience at least, many ethically- or religion-driven investors will not be open to shorting securities they would never allow to long.

6.2   Derivatives Instruments: The Case of Commodity Futures

Commodity futures are an example of a derivative security. Before we discuss these instruments in more detail, let's start by asking how sustainable investors should think about derivatives more broadly.

6.2.1   Derivatives in a sustainable portfolio

Derivatives are financial contracts the payoff of which depends on another asset (hence, derivatives). A classic example is a European put option, which gives you a right, but not an obligation, to sell a share of an underlying stock, at a prespecified price and at a prespecified time. For example, you may hold such an option to sell a share of Chevron at $100 on 17 May 2024. The $100 is referred to as the strike price, and 17 May 2024 is the maturity of the option. The option pays off if the price of Chevron is below the strike price at maturity. For example, if the stock is worth $90 on that day, being able to sell the stock at $100 is worth $10—you buy the stock in the open market for $90, and then exercise your put option to sell that same share at $100. Crucially, the option does not force you to sell. So, if the price at maturity is higher than $100, you do not need to do anything—the option expires worthless, but does not expose you to any additional cost.

Let's consider what ESG integration and impact look like with such a security. The example we will discuss is necessarily rather simplified. The point I want to drive is that sustainability can be useful for our understanding of risk and return of derivative securities such as this option (this should not be surprising by this stage of the book). I will try to do this by flashing out some of the intuition, with the caveat that there is much more to option pricing that we can consider here.[8]

The most obvious reason why ESG information may affect your view on the option is that it tells you something about the underlying asset. For example, if you believe that the market underestimates the importance of climate risks that Chevron may be exposed to, then you may have a view that the stock is overpriced. The price may fall in the future, possibly because the climate risk will materialize, or because the market will correct the initial mispricing (as we saw in Chapter 3, when the market views an asset as increasingly risky, the required rate of return may rise, and the asset's price will then fall). This may influence your view about the option: if the market does not appreciate the risks inherent in the underlying stock, it will also underprice the put option on that stock. Moreover, to the extent that the market underappreciates the risks of the stock (because it downplays its climate risk exposure), this, too, boosts the value of the option.

With higher risk, it is more likely that the stock price will be very low at the option's maturity. For example, the market may think that prices lower than, say, $80 per share are very unlikely, given its relatively low-risk estimate. You believe that the true risk of the stock is higher, which makes it more likely that the price will be as low as or lower than $80 at the option's maturity. We already know that this put option is worth more when the stock price is lower. If your view suggests that low prices are likelier than what the market believes, then the option is worth more, in your view, than what the market prices it at.

So, just as with stocks and bonds, we may be able to use sustainability to better understand the risk and return of derivative instruments. And, just as with more traditional instruments, we could trade derivatives to implement an investment view—for example, if you believe that a major climate repricing is imminent, you may want to buy the put option on an oil major, of the sort we described just now. At this point, you may wonder why even bother with derivatives, since you might as well trade the underlying stock (in this case, short it). It turns out, there are benefits to implementing a view using a derivative instrument. One such advantage is the leverage embedded in derivatives. Investing in derivatives gives you more exposure to the underlying investment idea than you might get if you invested directly in the underlying asset. With more exposure, if your investment idea pans out, then for each dollar you invest, your returns will be higher with the derivative than with the underlying. This is attractive for many investors, although, of course, there is no magic here—the opportunity for outsize returns simply means that you take on more risk. If your idea does not pan out, then your loss may be amplified as well. For example, if you allocate some of your capital to buy the put option, but the price of the stock increases, your option would expire worthless—that's a negative 100% return on the capital you invested.

Besides the higher exposure, derivatives may be easier and cheaper to trade, at least for institutional investors. This is perhaps most evident when structuring a complex trade, which requires buying and selling multiple securities. For a practical example, consider the Stranded Asset Swap developed by the World Wild Fund (WWF). WWF wanted to eliminate oil and gas exposure from its investment portfolio and designed a derivative instrument (the Swap) to do so. The idea of a financial swap is to exchange two streams of payments with a counterparty. WWF wanted to exchange the returns on assets they disliked (a basket of coal, tar sands, and oil and gas companies) for the returns on an asset they did like (a broad market index, and WWF selected the S&P 500 for that purpose). Using the terminology we introduced earlier in this chapter, they wanted to build a portfolio that goes long on the S&P 500 (earning them the return on the index) and short the basket of fossil fuel companies. If the S&P does better than the fossil fuel firms, then WWF earn a positive return on this strategy—which is likely what they experienced, given that they had the swap on between 2014 and 2021.[9] Of course, when fossil fuel firms do better than the broader market (as was the case, for example, in 2022), the swap will then lose money. This is precisely the payoff we'd look for if we wanted to hedge a fossil fuel exposure, or perhaps build a strategy that benefits from a shift toward renewables.

Having covered ESG integration with derivatives let's now talk about impact. Could trading a derivative instrument influence real-economy activities of companies and other economic actors? The framework we developed in Chapter 5 makes it clear that impact with derivatives is only possible through the financing cost channel. There is no control: derivatives may give you exposure to the price of a stock but do not grant you any voting rights or other forms of direct influence on the portfolio company. But how exactly would derivatives influence a firm's financing costs? After all, companies get capital from their issuance of stocks or bonds, not from derivatives based on these assets. So, derivatives can only influence financing costs if they can influence the price of the underlying security. Going back to our earlier example, if a put option on an oil major's stock affects the price of the stock (in this case, if it decreases it), then it also influences the oil major's cost of capital, which in turn critically affects the firm's capital budgeting and investment decisions.

This means that the question we need to answer is whether trading derivatives can possibly affect the price of the underlying stock. There are strong theoretical reasons why that is the case. When you trade a derivative instrument, you typically do so with a broker. The broker takes the opposite side of your trade and assumes the risks that come with it. Ideally, the broker would find a different investor interested in that opposite side, and offer them a mirror image of your contract (so, if you are buying a put, the broker would ideally find a different investor who's interested in selling that put). Failing that, the broker will typically hedge their exposure by trading in the underlying. So, if you bought a put option from the broker, the broker would hedge their exposure by shorting the underlying stock. And, as we already discussed, shorting the stock can impact the underlying company. In this specific case, the impact only arises because you bought the put in the first place, enticing the broker to short the stock. This is less direct than if you shorted the stock, but at the end of the day, it reflects the same economic mechanism.

In addition, the prices of the derivative and the underlying asset are tightly linked through potential arbitrage between the two. That is, if the price of a derivative changes but the price of the underlying does not, there will be an arbitrage opportunity (a chance to make a riskless profit) that market participants will pounce on. Once more, I refer the interested reader to a derivatives textbook, but here is a high-level example to illustrate this point. Suppose that we buy the put option we discussed earlier and that our trade is large enough to increase the price. This creates an opportunity for other market participants: they will try to sell the put at its now-higher price while hedging their position by shorting the underlying stock. This opportunity will last until the price of the put falls down to its earlier price, or until the price of the stock falls (or some combination of the two). The bottom line is that if our purchase of the put leads to a persistent increase in the price of the option, then the price of the underlying stock will be driven down, by the forces of arbitrage. As we will see in a moment, this may be a big "if," but if it is true, then trading the option will also have some impact on the underlying company's financing cost.

Having discussed a vanilla example of a derivative, let's now move on to the perhaps more interesting (and certainly more contentious) question of ESG integration and impact for commodity futures.

6.2.2   Commodity futures

First, what are commodity futures? They are derivative instruments, the value of which depends on the price of a physical commodity. Specifically, a futures contract obliges you to buy or sell that commodity at a prespecified price (the strike price) and on a prespecified date (the maturity of the contract). Historically, these instruments were valuable tools for producers and consumers of physical commodities to hedge their risks. The standard example introduces us to a farmer who produces wheat and to a miller who produces flour from the wheat they buy from the farmer. When the farmer decides how much wheat to sow, he or she takes a risk on the future price of the commodity. If the price is high at the time of the harvest, the farmer makes a profit; if the price is low, the farmer makes a loss. The miller has the opposite exposure: they will buy the wheat at harvest, and the lower the price of wheat, the larger their profit will be. Months before the harvest, both parties face this price risk. Being risk averse, they can enter into a binding contract that specifies the price they will transact at in the future. They can then plan ahead without worrying about price fluctuations in the meantime.

Commodity futures contracts we trade today are conceptually similar to the contract between the farmer and the miller. To be clear, there are many nuances here, including settlement (which may require taking physical delivery of the commodity, or just exchanging a financial payment equal to the difference between the strike price and the price prevailing at maturity), margin requirements, etc. For our discussion, we won't need to understand all these nuances, just the concept of getting exposure to the commodity price through a financial instrument.

Why would sustainable investors care about commodity futures? First, because these contracts may allow the investor to implement their investment views, which may well be ESG motivated. For example, an investor may have a view on the price of oil, perhaps because they expect a change in environmental policy or news about the transition to renewables. The investor may prefer not to implement that view by trading the physical commodity (which involves storage, etc.) or trading energy stocks (which gives exposure to more than just the price of oil). Instead, trading oil futures may be the most direct and the most efficient way to implement the view; the economic leverage inherent in futures could further make this a capital efficient way to boot. As another example, some investors may want to use weather data to build a view on the future price of agricultural commodities, and then use futures on these commodities to implement the view in their portfolios. In fact, some of the data examples we covered in Chapter 4 have a clear relevance for commodities. As you may remember, we discussed research linking droughts to agricultural production. In Chapter 4, we used that insight to discuss investing in the stock of food companies, but one can easily imagine designing a commodity futures strategy instead.

Of course, as we saw before, ESG integration is rarely questioned. It is the potential impact of commodity futures that makes these securities somewhat controversial. Think back to our example of an investor trading oil futures. Some commentators suggested that holding such contracts, or at least going long on such contracts, stimulates more production of the underlying asset—in this case, drilling for more oil. If this is true, then it would seem that investors holding such futures have a hand in increasing the supply of oil for the economy. And while energy is the most obvious area of concern, some have also questioned agricultural futures (since the rearing of, say, cattle may have implications for climate change, water management, etc.) or even precious metals (since some precious metals may be produced using child labor, etc.).

So, is there anything to the idea that trading commodity derivatives influences the spot market? The short answer is that we do not know. It is a controversial topic, with mixed evidence from academic researchers. To see an example of this tension, let me offer a somewhat dated case study here: the discussion about what drove the spike in oil prices in 2007–2008, and the congressional subcommittee hearings on this topic. One of the experts testifying in front of Congress was Fadel Gheit, a Senior Oil Analyst for Oppenheimer. Gheit testified that he believed that "the energy markets in recent years have been driven more by speculation than by industry fundamentals of supply and demand. Oil prices peaked in July at more than $148 [per barrel], despite softening demand, to more than double their levels a year earlier. Since then, oil prices declined by more than 36% despite supply disruptions. Speculation has disconnected oil prices from market fundamentals."[10] This is a strong statement, and definitely grist for the mill of proponents that financial derivatives can influence the spot market. However, this is not the only view. Paul Krugman disagreed in his *New York Times* article, stating that "regulating futures markets more tightly isn't a bad idea, but it won't bring back the days of cheap oil." Among other arguments, Krugman pointed out that other commodities also went up in price, even though there were no financial derivatives in play. For example, iron ore prices just about doubled over the period in question, but iron ore is not exchange traded—there are no iron futures. Krugman posited that the price increases simply reflected the market's anticipation of demand and supply in the spot market (i.e., in the market for physical commodities), regardless of whether there were financial derivatives on those commodities.[11]

Academic evidence is similarly split on the question. From a purely theoretical perspective, there may be some short-term, but probably not long-term feedback effects between financial derivatives and the spot market. Think back to our stylized example of a farmer and a miller contracting on the future price of wheat. If financial speculation pushes the futures price of wheat, then the farmer may be very eager to sign that contract, which would guarantee a higher price at harvest. The farmer may then want to plant more seeds, now that the price is higher than previously expected. However, sooner or later, the price of the commodity must be set by supply and demand. The higher price is good for the farmer, but bad for the miller. The miller is not willing to buy as much wheat at that price, which means that the market will not be in equilibrium. The additional supply the farmer has generated is not met by extra demand, which means that the price will fall. So, if there is an impact between the derivative and the spot market, that impact is probably relatively short-lived and will eventually be curbed by the supply of and the demand for the underlying physical commodity. But, for better or worse, the data is not clear enough to conclusively demonstrate impact even in the short term.[12]

My own view is most informed by onion futures. It is perfectly fine if you haven't heard about onion futures before—this interesting contract is, in fact, illegal in the United States. Things were different in the past. Onion futures were actually one of the more popular and most liquid commodity futures in the early twentieth century. In fact, they may have been too popular because, at some point, speculation in onion futures was deemed to destabilize the spot market. This is precisely the channel of impact we are discussing here. Onion farmers appealed to their representatives to remedy this situation, and in 1958 the Onion Futures Act was passed, banning trading in the eponymous contract. This is a fascinating story (even if only tangentially related to ESG investing), but the bottom line for us is what happened after the Act was passed. This was what researchers call a "quasi-natural experiment": an intervention that allowed them to compare the onion market with and without functioning onion futures. Not surprisingly, a number of researchers analyzed this case study for potential "before and after" effects. To my reading of the literature, the bottom line is that not much has changed. Perhaps the only quantity that was meaningfully different was the volatility of the spot price: onion prices became more volatile after onion futures were outlawed.[13] I do not know if increasing the volatility of the price of a commodity is necessarily in the broad interest of sustainable investors. Perhaps it is. But, even so, I would stress again that the empirical evidence is at best patchy.

The final piece of the puzzle is perhaps more conceptual. Even if we were convinced that trading financial derivatives can influence the spot price, it is not clear what the "sustainable" positioning may be. Take oil futures: would ESG investors prefer to short oil and potentially decrease spot oil prices, or long oil and potentially increase them? I would argue for the long side: with higher oil prices, consumers will have more economic incentive to look for non-fossil-fuel sources of energy, and perhaps will stimulate renewable businesses in the process. Similarly, consider the United Nations' Sustainable Development Goals (SDGs).[14] SDG 2 is "zero hunger," so you might feel it is aligned with a short position on agricultural commodities, potentially lowering food prices for consumers. That may be the case, but if so, this positioning may clash with SDG 1, "no poverty," because agricultural production is a source of income to a substantial portion of emerging countries' populations, and lower commodity prices may hurt their wellbeing. Is the tradeoff acceptable? Again, in the absence of conclusive empirical evidence, it may be difficult to take a strong stance on this question. My own view is that commodity derivatives are sufficiently divorced from the spot market that they are close to neutral on sustainability— neither good nor bad in terms of their potential impact.

The one exception I would allow is for a specific kind of commodity: carbon emissions and their associated derivative contracts, futures on carbon allowances.

6.2.3 Futures on carbon allowances

Carbon allowances are permits to emit greenhouse gasses within an Emissions Trading System (ETS). An ETS sets a total emissions cap that is usually declining over time, and regulated entities must surrender tradable carbon allowances to cover their emissions in a given year. Each allowance allows the company holding it to emit a prespecified amount of greenhouse gasses (e.g., a ton of CO_2-equivalent emissions). Companies within an ETS that cannot present enough allowances to cover all their emissions are fined; companies that hold more allowances than their emissions can sell the surplus to other ETS participants.

It may be worthwhile to highlight a distinction between carbon allowances and other related terms, "carbon taxes" or "carbon offsets." Carbon allowances set the level of emissions for covered industry sectors and allow the market to determine the price through trading between firms that emit more and need allowances, and firms that emit less and have a surplus. In contrast, carbon taxes set the price of carbon and then rely on economic agents to reduce emissions in reaction to the price. Lastly, carbon offsets are a very different concept. They refer to projects meant to remove greenhouse gases from the atmosphere or prevent further release of such gases (e.g., through preventing deforestation). While carbon allowances are mandated within an ETS, carbon offsets are, as of this writing at least, voluntary. They are often used by firms that wish to lower their carbon footprint, even if many commentators complain about the very inconsistent quality of most offsets currently available in the market. Over time, I would expect the quality to be more stringently enforced and eventually offsets may find a more widespread use in investment portfolios as well. In fact, the Chicago Mercantile Exchange has recently started trading carbon offset futures, and while this market is still nascent, it may, over time, gain more popularity.[15] After this quick aside, let's come back to carbon allowances which, unlike carbon taxes, are tradeable in investment portfolios and, unlike carbon offsets, are already a vibrant and liquid market.

There are a number of ETS systems around the world, but those that are of most interest to investors are arguably the European Union's ETS and the California Cap-and-Trade program. These systems are relatively large and liquid, and crucially they also have deep markets for carbon allowance futures. These instruments are similar to other derivatives we described in this chapter in that they give investors convenient access to the price of the underlying asset (the carbon allowance). Carbon allowance futures are typically included in the broader category of commodity futures, even though there are clear differences between a permit to emit greenhouse gasses and physical commodities such as, say, wheat or gold. And while we already discussed why an ESG-focused investor might be comfortable trading physical commodity futures, there are additional nuances involved in trading (futures on) carbon allowances.

As usual, we will start with ESG integration. Perhaps the most obvious reason why ESG-focused investors may want to invest in (futures on) carbon allowances is their desire to manage climate risk, particularly risks related to the transition to the low-carbon economy. Allowances are a natural tool to manage such risks, because they are the policy instrument that governments will leverage to facilitate the transition. Specifically, governments that want to speed up the transition will decrease the supply of allowances, which will then drive up the price of these instruments. This is bad news to browner companies, whose higher emissions cost more, and to producers of fossil fuels, whose products are now more expensive to use by their customers. Investors who hold such fossil fuel companies will likely experience negative returns. However, if these investors also hold futures on allowances, they will have an offsetting gain on those positions (since allowances increased in price).

Finally, let's think about the potential impact of trading futures on carbon allowances. As before, the key will be investors' ability to increase the price of the underlying allowances. If trading futures does that, then it also affects the real economy, through the same channel we already discussed. Interestingly, there is one more way that trading futures on carbon allowances may have impact. Recall that futures help commodity producers hedge price risks. Every year, they will need to surrender allowances that cover their emissions in that year. Normally, they would be able to hedge this risk by buying carbon allowance futures—they could lock in the price they need to pay months ahead of time. However, this time the firms compete with sustainable investors, who also want to buy the futures and thus take the same side of the transaction. This means that it will be more difficult, and perhaps more costly, for firms to hedge the cost of their future emissions, forcing them to be more conservative in their production plans. So, both the price and the hedging argument suggest that trading carbon allowance futures could indeed have some impact by making it more difficult for brown firms to emit as much as they otherwise would.

Notes

1. I am deliberately keeping this section focused on the interplay between shorting and sustainability and do not discuss concepts such as naked shorts.
2. See, for example, https://www.pionline.com/esg/oregon-treasurer-maps-plan-pension-fund-reach-net-zero
3. For example, see Krueger, P., Sautner, Z., and Starks, L.T. (2020). The importance of climate risks for institutional investors. *The Review of Financial Studies*, 33 (3): 1067–1111, https://academic.oup.com/rfs/article-abstract/33/3/1067/5735302
4. For a discussion of how difficult it is to reach net zero for a traditional investor, please see Palazzolo, Ch., Pomorski, L., and Zhao, A. (2022). (Car)bon voyage: the road to low carbon investment portfolios. In J. Zhang, ed., *Climate Change: Managing the Financial Risk and Funding the Transition*, Risk Books.

5. Grullon, G., Michenaud, S., and Weston, J.P. (2015). The real effects of short-selling constraints. *The Review of Financial Studies*, 28 (6): 1737–1767, https://doi.org/10.1093/rfs/hhv013

6. For more details on this issue, see Asness, C. (2022, 23 February). Shorting counts, AQR blog post, https://www.aqr.com/Insights/Perspectives/Shorting-Counts

7. For more information on this class of strategies, see: Thinking broadly: improving active performance via systematic extensions. Acadian working paper, https://www.acadian-asset.com/investment-insights/systematic-methods/thinking-broadly-improving-active-performance-via-systematic-extensions

8. The interested reader may want to consult Hull, J.C. and Basu, S. (2017). *Options, Futures, and Other Derivatives*, 10e. Pearson, for an overview. Those readers who are more technically inclined may also want to refer to Ilhan, E., Sautner, Z., and Vilkov, G. (2021). Carbon tail risk. *The Review of Financial Studies*, 34 (3): 1540–1571 for a discussion of option pricing with sustainability preferences.

9. As per the WWF website, https://www.worldwildlife.org/pages/supporting-the-future-of-conservation-how-we-manage-our-investments

10. The interested reader may want to consult the full transcript of that meeting, available at https://www.energy.senate.gov/public/index.cfm/files/serve?File_id=6CC02439-D267-385A-DC66-657321E66171

11. Krugman, P. (2008, 27 June). Fuels on the Hill. *The New York Times*, https://www.nytimes.com/2008/06/27/opinion/27krugman.html

12. For an elegant model that illustrates the potential short-term effect, see Knittel, C.R. and Pindyck, R.S. (2016). The simple economics of commodity price speculation. *American Economics Journal: Macroeconomics*, 8 (2): 85–110. For studies

that review the inconclusive empirical evidence, see, for example, Sanders, D.R. and Irwin, S. (2010). A speculative bubble in commodity futures prices? Cross-sectional evidence. *Agricultural Economics*, 41 (1): 25–32, https://doi.org/10.1111/j.1574-0862.2009.00422.x and Cheng, I.-H. and Xiong, W. (2014). Financialization of commodity markets. *Annual Review of Financial Economics*, 6 (1): 419–441.

13. For example, see Working, H. (1960). Price effects of futures trading. *Food Research Institute Studies*, 1 (1): 3–31.

14. See https://sdgs.un.org/goals

15. See for example https://www.cmegroup.com/media-room/press-releases/2022/2/08/cme_group_to_launchcblcore globalemissionsoffsetfutures.html

Chapter 7

Conclusions

We covered a lot of ground in this book. Across the previous five chapters, we built a foundation for how investors should think about sustainability. We covered how investors incorporate ESG and how their actions affect their portfolios' risk and return. We also discussed how markets react to and price ESG information. Importantly, this includes an analysis of how we should think about price changes around market transitions—say, a shift to a market where many investors have both financial and nonfinancial interests in ESG. We ventured into the treacherous terrain of ESG data, discussed impact through financial portfolios, and how to apply sustainability in alternative asset classes.

It is my hope that the book gave you multiple aha! moments and helped you understand and maybe even appreciate the many tradeoffs sustainable investors struggle with. I would be particularly pleased if our discussion moved you away from the extreme viewpoints that, unfortunately, dominate the conversation today. Yes, ESG is critically important and simply not negotiable for many investors, small and large, individuals and institutions. This does not mean, though, that it is the right solution for all investors and the panacea for the world's needs in financial markets and beyond. As I warned you in the introduction, the right answer to many important questions may indeed be "it depends."

Having said that, I hope that I gave you at least some tools to understand what "it" depends on. The intuition we have built is based on fundamental economic insights, which makes it more powerful and, hopefully, timeless. You'll need such tools and frameworks. This is still a very young field, and it is brimming with innovation. We had a chance to see some of the newish sustainable investing instruments, for example, green bonds in Chapter 5 or shorting and derivatives in Chapter 6. There are many more, and you should absolutely try to analyze them using a similar approach we pursued in this book. This also holds for ESG data, where seemingly every passing week brings a new product from one of the many data providers. Chapter 4 gave you a blueprint for how to think about data. If nothing else, I hope it left you with a conviction that due diligence is critical here.

Are there parts of this book that may not age well? Probably, but if I had known which ones, I would have written this book differently. I fully expect that our frameworks and the way of thinking about sustainable investing will hold as well going forward as they do today. But I do allow that there may be changes in the stylized empirical patterns I discussed in this book. Perhaps some of the many predictors of returns we've discussed will go out of favor, maybe because the market will finally learn how to price them in completely. And, who knows, maybe we will even see return predictability where we don't see it today. For example, when talking about ESG ratings, I was skeptical about their power to forecast future returns. I do believe that you may be able to outperform by using more nuanced and less obvious ESG insights, just not this most standard of ESG data. I stand by this assessment because I think markets today can be best described as "ESG aware" but perhaps not quite "ESG motivated." (If they were, I would expect more than just the relatively paltry green bond greenium that we currently see.) But markets are dynamic. If even more investors take on sustainable portfolio goals over time, then perhaps ESG ratings will eventually become important for expected returns. However, as we know from Chapter 3, they will do so in the opposite direction from what sustainable investors may wish (high ESG scores will predict poor returns). I do not think there is any evidence that this is already happening today, but it may in the future. And interestingly, there is a tantalizing ESG alpha opportunity even in this scenario. If you want to beat an

ESG-motivated market using ESG ratings, then the name of
the game will be not acting on the rating itself but rather trying
to predict future changes in the ratings. This is because when a
change occurs, sustainable investors will push prices as they
reposition their portfolios, selling the newly downgraded stocks
and purchasing the newly upgraded ones. If you are good at
predicting such changes, then you can capitalize on this subsequent repricing.

Finally, this is an interesting time to write a book about
ESG investing. After years of huge interest and substantial
inflows into sustainable strategies, there is a clear slowdown in
the trend. As I was writing these words, I saw a news report
showing that global sustainable flows turned negative in the last
quarter of 2023 for the first time on record.[1] (First time ever
globally: we saw quarters with negative ESG flows in specific
regions, for example, in the US in late 2022). Does this mean
that sustainable investing is over? Not by a long shot. First, we
are seeing a slowdown in flows, but even the most pessimistic
assessments of sustainable assets indicate at least $3 trillion
invested in sustainable strategies. Moreover, we now know that
ESG is not limited to those strategies that are necessarily ESG-
labeled. Many "ordinary" strategies unapologetically integrate
ESG insights in their positioning or trade ESG-related assets.
Their managers do so because it improves the strategy purely
from the risk–return standpoint. For example, as I mentioned
earlier in this book, 2023 saw the issuance of an estimated $900
billion in new labeled bonds. This means that there were enough
interested investors to provide this additional funding to the
issuers of green, social, or sustainability-linked bonds. We discussed other new instruments that matter for sustainable investors, for example, the innovative futures on carbon allowances.
The trading volume in the futures on European allowances is
nowadays in the billions of dollars trading daily.

So, ESG investing is not going away. We will have ample opportunity to argue about it in the future. I just hope we can start with a common understanding of the economic tradeoffs that portfolio management necessarily reflects. We may differ in our assessment of the evidence or in whether a tradeoff is worth it (does this increase in sustainability justify this drop in financial attractiveness?). But assessing the tradeoff will help us appreciate the other person's view. And if this book has nudged you in that direction, then I have achieved my goal.

Note

1. Bloomberg. (2024, 25 January). US investor exodus deals historic blow to global ESG fund market. https://www .bloomberg.com/news/articles/2024-01-25/sustainable-funds-see-first-ever-global-quarterly-net-outflows

Index

Page numbers followed by *f* refer to figures.